**THE PENTATONIC PRESS INTEGRATED LEARNING SERIES**
Teaching The Whole Child Through Music: Language Arts

# Intery Mintery
## NURSERY RHYMES
For Body, Voice and Orff Ensemble

T0294424

**DOUG GOODKIN**

## OTHER BOOKS BY DOUG GOODKIN

+ *All Blues: Jazz for Orff Ensemble:* Pentatonic Press: 2012
+ *The ABC's of Education: A Primer for Schools to Come:* Pentatonic Press: 2006
+ *Now's the Time: Teaching Jazz to All Ages:* Pentatonic Press: 2004
+ *Play, Sing & Dance: An Introduction to Orff Schulwerk:* Schott Publishers; 2002
+ *Sound Ideas: Activities for Percussion Circle:* Alfred Publishing 2001
+ *Name Games: Activities for Rhythmic Development:* Alfred Publishing 1998
+ *A Rhyme in Time: Rhythm, Speech Activities and Improvisation for the Classroom:* Alfred Publishing 1997
+ *Teach Like It's Music: An Artful Approach to Education:* Pentatonic Press 2019

For further information, go to: www.douggoodkin.com

Cover Design: Sue Sandlin Design
Cover Artwork: Rebecca Story
Photographs: Cristiana Ceppas, Doug Goodkin, Mark Johann, Nate Keck, Sofía López-Ibor, Jean Makanna. All photos of children from The San Francisco School.
Editor: Peter Greenwood
Book design and typesetting: Bill Holab Music
ISBN Number: 0–9773712–2–0

# TABLE OF CONTENTS

**Advanced Arrangements—3rd to 5th Grade**

# PREFACE

It was time to get ready for our annual Halloween ceremony at school. The children came into class and as they were removing their shoes, I played a pattern on a drum. I hadn't played for more than twenty seconds when my student James said in one big breath:

> "Oh, I know what you're playing. That's the part that goes with the *Intery Mintery* song and the third graders play it, well, not all the third graders, just one of them, I think it was Mark last year, and he doesn't play the drum, but those two bass bars and that big cymbal and then we're going to play those bamboo rattles up there, well, some of us are, others are going to be sitting over there with brooms which Sofia keeps over in the corner there and there's a black light and then they take the brooms away and make a face, except some of them have those fans that are painted that are over by the desk and..."

James is seven years old. He experienced this celebration *once*, an entire year ago. It obviously made an impression.

This book is about the things that capture children's imagination and speak to their heart—rhymes, poetry, music, dance, stories and celebration. In these pages we will see how such things are also good food for the brain, training the mind to recognize and understand the structures that permeate language and music and give them both the power of articulation. We will experience how nursery rhymes can help develop musical skill and understanding and how music can animate language study.

Come join me as we travel through 48 tried-and-true activities drawn from 34 years of work at The San Francisco School, journeying from the single phoneme to the full-blown *Intery Mintery* celebration that so captured young James' imagination. Along the way, we'll meet a cast of colorful characters, get a solid foundation in the music pedagogy of Orff Schulwerk, consider a model of sequential development in both language and music and enliven our classes so that they're more engaging for children and teachers alike.

A book is a difficult medium in which to transmit this information, lacking the full dimensions of the experience itself. But it has been a pleasure to gather many years of work between two covers in the hope that these activities and ideas might be useful for your program. Like any such venture, it has come into being through the helping hands of numerous people—the children who played and helped shape these arrangements, the constant affirmation, challenge and inspiration from my two brilliant colleagues, Sofía López-Ibor and James Harding and the relentless commitment to the music program from The San Francisco School. Thanks are due to the "Pentatonic Press team"—to Bill Holab for layout and design, Sue Sandlin for the cover design, Sofía López-Ibor for collecting photos and general advice, and to Corrine Olague for proofreading. Thanks to Rebecca Story and Shireen Teheranian for the cover art work and to Talia Goodkin for her imaginative re-working of some of this material. The largest thanks goes to my editor Peter Greenwood, who roped and saddled the wild horses of my excessive writing and brought them into the corral of coherence.

I don't remember my mother bouncing me on my knee to nursery rhymes, but when I was two, she brought me into a little booth in New York City and recorded me reciting *Humpty Dumpty*. I still have the record. My father later shared his own love affair with language, teaching me to do Crostic puzzles and introducing me to a few choice poems he liked to recite. And so I dedicate this book to the memory of my father, S. James Goodkin and the constant comfort of my mother, Florence Goodkin.

# INTRODUCTION

It's an old story: twins separated in infancy are joyfully reunited and live happily ever after. That's the theme of this book—language and music, after so many years in separate classrooms, are brought together again and rejoice in discovering their forgotten parts—the music of language and the language of music. They sit, play and dance side-by-side once more, enjoying each other's company throughout their school days.

Before we understand how to work with language and music together in our lessons, we first need to consider their twin nature. One useful key is the four S's:

**SOUND**—In both language and music, sound hits the ear first. We immediately distinguish between German, French or Chinese, between a string quartet, gamelan or percussion section. The sensuality of sound brings a musical lilt to language that gives us pure pleasure in words separate from (and in addition to) their meaning.

**SYLLABLE**—This is the language equivalent of rhythm in music, attending to both beat groupings and accent. Along with sound, it taps on our innate pleasure in rhythm and refreshes us with its metrical music.

**SENSE**—Here music and language begin to separate. The prime purpose of language is to make sense of the world, to describe, communicate and record our experience. Music must also make sense, but not in the same way—it speaks the language of emotion, not ideas, articulating our experiences before words begin and after they leave off. When joined in song, each kind of sense amplifies the other.

**STORY**—Language gives concrete names to the things in our world—pansy, paintbrush, politician—and describes abstract relationships—Botany, Impressionism, Democracy—but its highest purpose is storytelling. From the news of the day at the dinner table to elaborate mythologies, stories give us the characters, images and situations that frame our sense of meaning. Music is a kind of storytelling as well, setting up its characters and conflicts in its opening, taking them through the drama of development in the middle and giving us a sense of resolution at the end.

Nursery rhymes are the perfect way to begin a formal study of both language and music. They are carefully crafted in their *sound*, leaning heavily on the poetic devices of rhyme, alliteration, assonance, onomatopoeia and beyond. They draw attention to *syllable* in their rhythmic expression and tune our ear to meter and phrasing. They help us decipher the meaning of words old and new (what exactly is a clinker that Tommy Tinker sat on?), to make *sense* of each rhyme even when it is nonsense. They lead us into history and tour us around culture. And most intriguing to the children, they tell us little *stories* that help us wend our way through the world, sympathizing with the robin hiding from the storm or dancing in our imagination with the dish and the spoon.

**How *Intery Mintery* Is Organized**

The book is divided into two sections. The first part features activities scored for voice, body percussion and movement and requires nothing more than a teacher, a group of students and an active imagination. The activities progress in a logical development from phoneme to poem and demonstrate the dynamic teaching process that characterizes Orff Schulwerk (see my book *Play, Sing and Dance: An Introduction to Orff Schulwerk* listed in the bibliography). Those new to the Orff approach will get a good feeling for how it works simply by trying the activities as described.

The second section features rhymes arranged for the Orff instrument ensemble. These fully realized arrangements with distinct melodies and accompanying parts offer set pieces playable by children of all ages. They are arranged to model a logical melodic-harmonic sequence for children from pre-school through 5th grade. Pieces are grouped across grades to suggest flexibility— a piece I normally do with first grade might work perfectly well with kindergarten or second grade.

This book is intended for both music and classroom teachers. Each will come to it with different backgrounds, different goals and thus, different outcomes. What might be helpful for each to know before diving into these pages?

**The Classroom Teacher**

As the teacher most responsible for leading children into literacy, you need a considerable repertoire of ideas, materials and strategies. The first section gives you generative ideas and concrete activities that animate language through music, movement and musical speech. The models are simple enough to understand and lead with no prior music training. And though some examples are notated, you do not need to read music to decipher the rhythm of a rhyme—simply read it aloud and chances are that you'll be correct.

The next section of the book focuses on the musical side of things and you may feel intimidated by esoteric vocabulary—*pentatonic, ostinato, polymeter*? Don't despair—these are simple concepts to grasp and worthy of attention. And though you're not likely to have the time, background or the instruments to play the Orff ensemble arrangements, there are still many riches worth mining. Three suggestions to help you through that part of the book:

+ Leave aside the Orff arrangement and look at what the rhyme itself suggests. Many of these could be excellent springboards into writing assignments ("The Mystery of the Lion and the Unicorn," "Moments When I Hid My Head Under My Wing," "From Peter Piper to Gerard Manley Hopkins" etc.). Some will be great for math class (*St. Ives, The House That Jack Built, Sally II*), some for history class (*Humpty Dumpty*), some for social skills (*The Owl*) and all worthy of the children's attention. Simply reciting them is often enough.
+ Share this book with your music teacher and collaborate.
+ Consider taking an Orff summer class. (See Appendix)

**The Music Teacher**

Those familiar with Orff Schulwerk will find ready examples of familiar processes and ideas, but may wish to note some details before going straight to the material itself. Those encountering the Orff approach for the first time will likely spend more time examining the process of arriving at the piece and considering the compositional style. In either case, there is enough material to see you through several years of classes.

These miniature works are the *starting* point for more extensive investigation by children and teacher alike. Throughout the book, I suggest that you think further than playing the pieces as written. Adapt them, change them, extend, supplement, improvise within them, dance and dramatize them.

The Schulwerk emphasizes the artistry of teaching and part of its challenge is to understand precisely how, when and why to make changes.

Some general suggestions are given here on preparing the pieces. They are specific enough to give you direction, but open enough to allow you to discover other possibilities with the children.

## Form

Most of these pieces feature simple forms with variations within the repetitions. A typical piece begins with a layering of drones and ostinati, alternates singing with playing, separates metals and woods in the playing and perhaps includes an unpitched percussion interlude. I have chosen not to write out the details of the form for three reasons:

1. If all the details were written out, each piece would be several pages long.
2. Forms are changeable and open-ended and it is assumed the teacher has an understanding of the basic procedures given above.
3. A companion recording presents one version of the form. (Available separately at www.douggoodkin.com)

## The Sequenced Curriculum

Each of the settings offered here are little worlds unto themselves. But they are also arranged in this book—and in my teaching as well—to demonstrate a progression from simple to complex, a sequenced curriculum, with each piece building from the skills, techniques and concepts of the one previous.

Four criteria used for sequencing:

1. From the phoneme to the poem in Part 1, moving through increasingly larger units of speech.
2. From simple to complex in the Orff arrangements of Part 2, with increasing challenges in technique, tempo, rhythm, melody, texture, etc.
3. From the two-note melody over the drone to pentatonic modes, transposition, transposed modes and more, building in melodic and harmonic concepts.
4. From the whimsical rhyme to the profound poem, with increasingly sophisticated texts.

Though you may pick and choose pieces in any order, the model of development is well worth examining. By presenting the pieces in sequence, we steadily enlarge the student's grasp of the fundamentals of music.

## Bold, Extravagant Language and Outrageous Images

As effective as the developmental structure is, it is only the supporting pillar of the house—what counts the most is who lives inside. Let's not forget to sit down and take tea with Mother Goose's eccentric offspring. This is our chance to let our imagination run wild (a cow jumping over the moon?), relax our moral uprightness (good for you, Georgie Porgie, kissing all those girls!), defer our politeness to honesty ("I do not like thee, Doctor Fell") and give voice to our defiance (" 'Baloney!' said Salome and she kicked the chandelier"). Since children are extravagant creatures, why not invite them to explore the less-civilized side of the rhymes, through babbled speech, dramatic recitation and exuberant movement? Be careful not to get so wrapped up in the details of this drone or that ostinato that you lose the wild side.

Meanwhile, as every parent and teacher knows, children need a certain amount of domestication—training in basic table manners, impulse control, deferred gratification, a habit of cleaning up after themselves—those little and big gestures that glue society together. They also need clear structures to hang their intuitive understandings on.

By combining the extravagant imagination of nursery rhymes with the scientific precision of acoustic principles and compositional techniques, both the wild and the domestic are honored and brought into conversation with each other.

Teachers also need to keep some of their own child-like extravagance alive in their classroom. My comments on the pieces are sometimes edgy (*The House That Jack Built*) or far-fetched (*Mother Caught a Flea*) or critical (*Old Man Mosie*), but all come leaping out from the bit of wild that I try to keep alive and healthy in my own teaching. The natural habitat of my class includes sitting barefoot in a circle, exuberantly chanting and proclaiming, unleashing a bit of percussive pandemonium and whirling and twirling joyfully around the room. I hope some of that feeling will come through in these pages and give you permission to move beyond tame classroom objectives.

# PART I: SPEECH, MOVEMENT, AND BODY PERCUSSION

## Language Arts Activities for All Ages

Language begins in the womb. Here, we are already absorbing the sounds that will become our mother tongue and the tones of voice that signal emotion. Once out into the world, we learn the power of the voice to express our needs, as we cry for milk or whimper in discomfort. In our calmer infant moments, we listen to the sounds around us and begin to imitate them—especially the sounds and words of our mother's voice. Step by step, we babble our way to our first "Mama!" and when we see our mother's delighted response, we know we're on to something. From the babbled phonemes, words begin to form and from single words to combinations, short phrases, sentences, and on to complete paragraphs and pages of communication.

Our first forays into language are supremely musical, that is to say, we are fascinated just by the *sound* of the words. Later on, we become more concerned about their meaning—"Hot!" "Want cookie!" "Your taxes are due by April 15th." But if we are lucky, we keep our love of the sound of speech our whole lives. Sound and rhythm are the "arts" side of the language arts curriculum and if we do our job well, we'll keep the trio of sound, syllable and sense dancing together. That's what all good poets, writers and speakers do.

This section is designed for all ages to re-animate the dance of language by literally dancing it, re-tuning our ear to the music of language by treating it musically. Music and dance teachers will shape the results toward more artful music and dance, while classroom teachers may use these as engaging entry points into some of the nuts and bolts of language—phonemic awareness, syllabic identification, parts of speech, alliteration, assonance, rhyme and a host of other details that all children must come to know and master. The last few activities lean more toward the musical side, in preparation for Part 2 of the book.

## 1. WHAT'S YOUR NAME? Phonemes, consonants, vowels, and a guessing game

All teachers need to learn their students' names, but why simply read the roll book? Here is a great opportunity for language and musical study alike. I have written extensively on that in *Name Games: Activities for Rhythmic Development* (Alfred Publishing), so here I am presenting just three activities.

In the linguistic journey from phoneme to fluency, from the sheer pleasure of shaped sound to the glories of Shakespeare, we begin with the most basic unit of language and work our way up. This not only helps children enter language at its musical foundation, but also helps them enter music through the familiarity of their mother tongue—and, in this case, from something intimate, personal, and uniquely theirs (even when others share the same word)—their name. "What's in a name?" queried an old bard and below are several of many musical answers to that timeless question.

### FIRST GAME: Puddin' Tane

*What's your name?*

*Puddin' Tane. Ask me again and I'll tell you the same.*

+ To a pat-clap beat, partners divide the above rhyme. Partner A asks, "*What's your name?*" and partner B answers as above.
+ Partner B then speaks the first sound of his/her name five times and A tries to guess name. If they guess correctly, switch roles and repeat rhyme. (If they don't guess after four tries, reveal your name.)

> Ex.   A) *D-d-d-d-d*   B) *DAN?*      A) *D-d-d-d-d*   B) *DERECK?*
>
> A) *D-d-d-d-d*   B) *DOMINIC?*   A) *D-d-d-d-d*   B) *DOUG?*

+ All face center. One speaks sound as above, partner reveals name, whole group repeats:

> (solo) *D-d-d-d-d-Doug* (Group) *D-d-d-d-d-Doug*

+ Continue around the circle as above.

### SECOND GAME: Pass the Phoneme

+ All seated in a circle, recite the Puddin' Tane rhyme once (optional beginning).
+ At the end of the rhyme, leader passes the first sound of his or her name to the beat with a gesture to the neighbor on the left. That person passes the sound of his or her name; continue this way around the circle. (For example, if the first four people were Dan, Alice, Fernando and Tanisha, it would be Duh-Aah-Fuh-Tuh).
+ When it returns to the leader, recite name again and pass sounds to the right.
+ Continue with variations (some examples below)

> Two sounds per beat    Duh-Duh  Aah-Aah  Fuh-Fuh  Tuh-Tuh
>
> Two sounds, two beats    Duh    Duh    Aah    Aah  Fuh   Fuh, etc.

+ As above; halfway through the circle, send one sound per beat to "catch up."
+ Pass the phoneme dramatically without any given beat, treating it as an object passed from hand to hand (while still speaking the sound). Choose from amongst the following qualities (or add your own): *something heavy/ delicate/ smelly/ slippery/ hot/ secret/ sexy/ a balloon flicked in the air, etc.*

### THIRD GAME: Consonants and Vowels

+ Leader creates percussive vocal pattern (ostinato) with first sound of name. If the name begins with a vowel, use the first consonant in the name ("L" for Alanna). Next person joins in with a contrasting or complimentary ostinato. Continue around the circle. In this exercise, try to eliminate all vowel sounds, clicking, popping and spitting out the consonant sound in the most percussive manner possible, using just the mouth, teeth and tongue. Without the aid of the voice box, each sound should be relatively quiet, but the group sound will be audible enough to be satisfying.

+ Half circle recites the *Puddin' Tane* poem, the other half answers by performing their consonant ostinati for 16 beats. Switch.
+ All create a melodic ostinato using the first vowel in their name (E for both Erin and Rebecca). Perform in half groups as shown above, alternating with rhyme.
+ Group according to first sounds of names and each group creates an ostinato using their sound. Ben, Bernard and Beatrice will create a percussive ostinato, Oscar and Olive a melodic one.
+ For those "one of a kind" people that don't have a group (Talia, Gail and Jasper/ Elijah, Aidan and Uma), create an ostinato by combining sounds. Select two to four groups to perform together. Example:

# Name Ostinati

**Comments**

As in many activities presented here, there are multiple levels at play and all need not be attempted in one class. Language arts teachers will be excited to consider a fun and musical approach to animating phonemes, consonants, and vowels and music teachers will have found an organic way to introduce rhythm and melody, staccato and legato, percussion and wind instruments, plucked strings and bowed strings, click sounds and sustained sounds, the building blocks of all music to come. As in just about everything we will do in these pages, the children are not just passively receiving information, but actively shaping it through a creative process. Sometimes they will improvise and compose by themselves to discover their own capabilities and sometimes in groups to enjoy the energy and collective imagination others provide. The foundation of the whole enterprise is the chance to play, explore, try things out—and have a heck of a good time doing it!

## 2. ICE CREAM SODA: Letter shapes, spelling, verbs and aerobic exercise

"Ice cream soda, Delaware punch,
Tell me the name of your honeybunch.
A-B-C-D-E-F-G..."

Do you remember this jump rope chant from your childhood? Such tension as you jump for all you're worth to get to the end of the alphabet and scoot out after Z, relieved that you don't have to confess your secret crush or be teased because you "love Paul or Paula." The game is simple—if you miss a jump during the alphabet section, the letter you stopped on is the first letter of your "honeybunch's" name—for less experienced jumpers, it might be Alice or Bruce, the more practiced ones, Wanda or Xavier. If you miss during the first part of the poem, simply start again until you reach the alphabet.

Sadly, it may be that many children won't be able to say, "Oh, I used to play that!" Instead, they'll say, "I think I saw something like that on a video game." Rather than leave it to chance, today's classroom, music, and P.E. teachers should get out the ropes and make sure that no child is left unjumped!

Meanwhile, this worthy activity, complete unto itself, also becomes a jumping off point, as it were, to an intriguing group movement exercise that enhances letter formation, spelling skills, group cooperation and makes verbs truly become action words.

### Part One: Letter formation

+ All jumping alone while reciting the chant together. Upon missing, they form the letter they missed on with the rope and also form that shape with their own body. When all have finished, play again.
+ Vary the above with body letter shapes flat on the ground. Then sitting, then standing.
+ As above in groups of three, two turning and one jumping. All three make the letter with the rope and then form the letter with their bodies together. They can choose a flat, sitting or standing shape—or combination of all three. Repeat with new jumper.

### Part Two: Spelling

+ Putting the ropes aside, groups of three perform a simple clap play while reciting (pat knees, clap hands, pat neighbor's hands on either side, clap own hands). On the word "honeybunch," each instantly forms a letter (two children consonants, one a vowel). They order themselves to spell a word—*cat, dog, rat, tar, bad, wet, tin, bug, ant, and, the,* etc. (Emphasize that they can't plan it ahead of time—it should be a surprise.)
+ Write down words they spell to form a master list. Can they see other possibilities for the same letters—*bad, dab/ tin, nit/ ten, net/ ant, tan/ rat, tar, art* etc.? (The ability to arrange and rearrange letters to form words is the key to success in the game *Boggle.*)

### Part Three: Verbs

+ Join two groups of three to make one of six. Drawing from scraps of paper in a basket, each group chooses a verb. They must spell the word with their bodies. Some letters may be made by one person, others by two or more. Suggested verbs include: *run, walk, swing, sway, grow, melt, push, pull, hop, erase, draw, blow, park (the car).*
+ After forming a word, each group must enact its meaning (run while in the letter shapes *run,* gradually dissolve the word *melt,* etc.).
+ Groups perform one at a time. This can be done in silence, teacher may accompany with live or recorded music or the group itself can make sound effects and/or sing a song (a waltz for *swing,* ascending scale for *grow,* etc.).

**Comments**

This latter activity never fails to deliver stunning little performances and elicit "oohs" and "aahs" from those observing. Some are funny, some energetic, some poignant and all bring the action of a verb to life in imaginative and refreshing new ways. Naturally, the sequence described above can be paced according to your needs, spread out over several classes or put together in one long class. For variety, try this older rhyme from England: "*Black currant, red currant, raspberry tart. Tell me the name of your sweetheart.*"

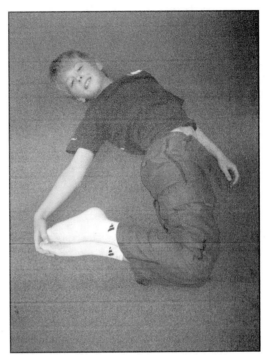

4th graders making letter shapes and spelling words.

# Choco-la-te

Chilean Children's Game

Pat front of partner's hands to the beat on "cho-co cho-co" (two beats for the four syllables)
Pat back of partner's hands to the beat on "La la"
Touch fists together to the beat on "te te"
Hands follow the pattern of the words
(front front back back front front fist fist front back front fist front back fist)
As above for "Mariposa" (butterfly), pointer fingers and thumbs touching on "sa-sa" instead of fists

## 3. CHOCO-LA-TE: Syllables, word, homonyms and a tasty pattern

Traveling around Chile, I happened upon two girls playing this game. I immediately rushed over and asked them to teach it to me (while their mother looked on a bit anxiously from the window). This simple game, probably found in other South American countries as well, is typical of the way children naturally develop their own language and math "curriculum." Though they won't talk with their friends about syllable recognition and discerning pattern, that is precisely what they are doing. In the music education world, there is currently a similar version that goes like this:

"Double double this this, double double that that,
Double this double that, double double this that."

### Teaching process

*Choco-la-te* has joined my bag of tricks for beginning a workshop. It creates an atmosphere of mystery, gets people connected, awakens their rhythm and gets their minds dressed for a workout in brain gym. The process goes something like this:

### Introduction/warm-up

+ Palms facing out expressing the beat in the air while speaking: ch ch ch ch (two sounds for each beat). After 16 beats turn the hands around and click tongue to the beat.
+ As above, with 8 beats each.
+ When pattern is firmly established, add one more beat gesture with fists, whistling one sound per beat. Settle into 8 ch ch's, 8 tongue clicks, 8 ch ch's, 8 whistles.
+ As above, with four of each. With two. With one. End with "ch ch click whistle" slowing down until one final, long whistle.

- Repeat above process with animal sounds—chicken, dog, chicken, cat.
- Gesture to the group to suggest new sounds and try out the suggestions.
- Repeat one more time with the syllables of "choco-la-te."
- Explore variations: hands on knees; in air facing up; on neighbor's back, etc.

Note that throughout this entire process there is no spoken explanation. This kind of "silent" teaching (speaking through gesture and sound rather than words) sharpens the attention of the students, creates an intriguing atmosphere and is a more musical way to teach than a constant drone of verbal explanation.

### The Game

- With partners, practice the text and gestures as shown in the notated version, touching partner's hands with each gesture.
- Turn around to new partner and practice "mariposa." ("butterfly" in Spanish)
- Increase tempo. Can play as an "out" game—partners sit down when they make a mistake. Last one standing is the winner.

### Extensions

- Figure out new word according to the model. For example, "alligator"—"*alli-alli-ga-ga-alli-alli-tor-tor-alli-ga-alli-tor-alli-ga-tor.*"
- Partners choose a new word with new motions and divide it according to the model. It's best not to explain the rules, but observe if they understand that the word must have four syllables with the accent on the first syllable ("communicate" doesn't work) and if they follow the pattern. Note that motions should relate to the word as much as possible while also connecting to the partner—like coffee-making or coffee-drinking gestures for "cappuccino." Some words suggest some homophonic interpretations rather than literal ones—for example, "television" might suggest touching each other's shins on the last syllable, "fettuccini" might suggest touching knees, "crocodile" feigning death on the third syllable.
- If the group numbers less than 30, have partners share their creations. If the group is larger, divide into quarters and have each section share.
- To further extend the activity, small groups create ostinati based on "chocolate." They can change the order of the syllables, repeat some syllables or vary the rhythm.
- Choose one or more to accompany the traditional game.

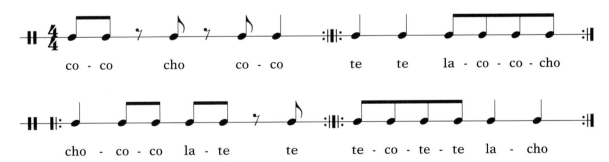

## COMMENTS: From Phoneme to Syllable to Word

From the phoneme of the name games, we move to the syllables within a single word. Building up from the bottom of language step-by-step, we recapitulate the child's journey into coherent speech and articulate language. Like the infant's initial experiments, we play our way into understanding and mastery. This approach characterizes all the activities in this book and as such, merits special comment. For though teachers seek quality material that speaks for itself, the Orff approach suggests that *how* we present the material is as important, if not more so, as *what* we present. And the "hows" are best understood by the teacher if accompanied by some solid "whys."

### The Cycle of Learning

Some wise teacher once remarked that if we want to talk about *this*, we begin by talking about *that*, leading the listener around the house and then unexpectedly entering through the side door. Note that in *Choco-la-te*, we didn't begin with the game itself, but instead, prepared the ground with a playful activity. This warms up the group and sets the musical flow in motion. By learning in silence, the student's mind has to work harder to figure out the patterns and that produces a deeper learning. The first stage of this process is playing around, exploring the territory, getting an intuitive feel for where we are before pulling out the map.

The second stage is the game itself, with its right and wrong answers and its precise form and technique. Though still playful (it is a game, after all), the sense of work creeps in, a feeling that we have to practice to get it right.

The third stage is taking what we've learned and creating something new with it. It has the playful feeling of the first stage, but now attends to the given form and structure.

Much music education concerns itself solely with the second stage, beginning with the activity itself and stopping at mastery of the given song, game or piece. The Orff approach not only prepares the activity with the kind of playful exploration modeled here, but also extends it beyond mere mastery. Each thing we learn is both complete in itself and also a stepping-stone to further invention. By finding a new word and motion, the learning becomes more deeply embedded and more conscious. And the pleasure of creating with others brings an exciting buzz to the class.

In planning a lesson, consider this threefold process:

    1) A playful period of exploration that leads to the main activity.

    2) A period of practice to master the activity.

    3) A creative re-interpretation or extension of the activity.

### Further Extensions

The above sequence is a refreshing cycle that feels complete when people have shared their words. But there are many other paths to further investigation. Where would you like to go?

**Language**: Use *Choco-la-te* as a jumping off point for syllable study and accent. If the children come up with some gestures as in the "fettuccini" example, follow their lead and begin your study of homonyms—die/dye, row/roe, do/dew, etc..

**Foreign language**: Draw from the language base in the classroom and learn four-syllable words in other languages. (This is a perfect game for international teaching that levels the playing field and enriches the results. In my own teaching, I learned the Finnish word for spider, a beautiful musical sound, "hamahake.")

**Music**: Notate the text with eighth, quarter notes and rest. Choose three tones to follow the form and create a little melody.

**Math**: Represent the pattern with three shapes:

⬜⬜⬜⬜△△⬜⬜⬜⬜ ⬜ ⬜⬜△⬜⬜ ⬜ ⬜⬜△ ⬜

**Art**: Make a collage of images following the pattern.

**Physical Education**: Create an exercise routine based on the pattern. Jump jump stretch stretch, jump jump kick kick, jump stretch, jump kick, jump stretch kick!

**History**: Research the story of chocolate.

Well, you get the idea. As John Muir said, "once we try to pick out anything by itself, we find it hitched to everything else in the universe." It's not likely that you would build a semester study around this little game—but somehow it's important to know you could.

# Criss Cross Applesauce

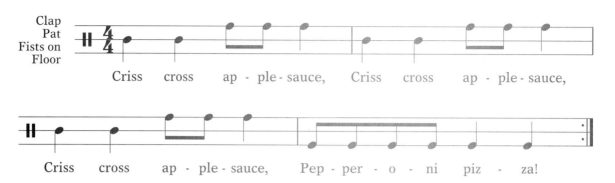

Speak twice, play with body percussion twice, speak and play twice and freeze into a shape.
Perform as four-part canon, entering every two beats.

## 4. CRISS CROSS APPLESAUCE: Vocal range and inclusive foods

This is one I learned from the kids, their name for the cross-legged style of sitting. In the first year of my teaching career, I crossed the line from desperate to manageable when I had the good fortune to visit P.E. teacher Rudy Benton's class. Amidst his many gifts of how to focus a class and conduct the group energy like a well-crafted orchestral performance came a vocabulary for sitting postures. There was long sitting, hook sitting, butterfly sitting, kneel sitting and their many variations (half-hook, half-long/ open long sitting, closed/side kneel-sitting, etc.). I learned how to begin actively with a parade (follow the leader) or a folk dance and get the kids into a circle. Then as soon as we sat down, off we went in a playful review of sitting postures, ending with the solid crossed-leg sitting that Mr. Benton called "tailor sitting." And tailor sitting it was for several decades—until kid culture came to The San Francisco School and suddenly we were sitting "criss cross applesauce."

This simple rhyme was a music teacher's dream! For now we not only had a musical language to catch kids' ears, the tick-tock, click-clack, hip-hop play of "criss-cross," the delicious (and nutritious) rhyme of "applesauce" and the alliterative festival of "p's" in pepperoni pizza, but we also had a perky, playable rhythm and a simple, kid-friendly form. What could go wrong?

Well, without experience or a clear plan, just about everything! But a little guidance goes a long way, so take a look at one of many ways to begin with a simple saying for sitting and turn it into a three-course meal of musical magic.

## Musical Development of Criss Cross
- After playfully reviewing various sitting postures, end with "criss cross applesauce" and energetically chant the rhyme twice through with the children. As shown in the score, use middle, high and low voices, taking care to match the vocal qualities with facial expression (especially eyebrows) and body posture.
- Pat, clap and play with fists on the floor the rhythm of the text twice through.
- Say and play the text together twice through, ending with a dramatic freeze on the final "-za!"
- As above, beginning in a whisper and performing as a gradual crescendo through the six repetitions.
- If the children are experienced enough, try the above in two part-canon, entering on 3rd beat (after "cross"). Four-part canon entering on 2nd beat (after "criss").
- Invite some children into the center of the circle to listen, with eyes closed, to the words, claps, and pats swirling around them in a whirlpool of sound.
- As above, changing the order of the canon. Those in middle guess.

**Say, Play, Say & Play**

This simple formula of say a text, play a text (while thinking the words) then saying and playing together accomplishes many things at once.

1) It extends a short rhyme into a more musical form with theme and variations.

2) It strengthens children's ability to internalize material by "saying it in their head." The Kodaly Method calls this "inner hearing," music educator Edwin Gordon calls it "audiation." Some musicians can hear all the parts (not just the text) in their head, but whether you are so gifted or not, it is a skill that can be strengthened through practice.

3) It connects hand and voice, teaching rhythm through language rather than abstract mathematical constructs. As shown in the name game activity, this technique of learning rhythm through speech has proven extremely effective and is affirmed by the rhythmic practices of India, West Africa and other cultures. "If you can say it, you can clap it" is the operating principle here.

You won't want to subject every text to this formula, but the process reaps great results. Try it and see.

**Variations**

- Invite alternative endings based on other foods people enjoy. The rhythm must be the same as "pepperoni pizza" and the rule of alliteration must prevail. Some examples:
  "Sushi and sashimi."
  "Beef and bean burritos."
  "Tantalizing tofu."
  "Cauliflower curry."

- Following the ideas of separating vowels and consonants in our name game, speak just the vowels in the rhyme, creating ostinati from the consonants, as shown here:

## Criss Cross Applesauce

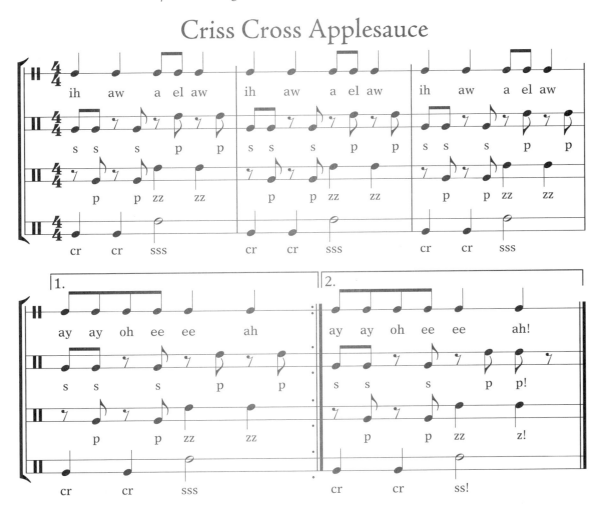

◆ Another version of the simple criss cross rhyme found its way into Orff circles and thence, to my classroom. Here it is, in all its sensual delight:

# Criss Cross—Tickle Version

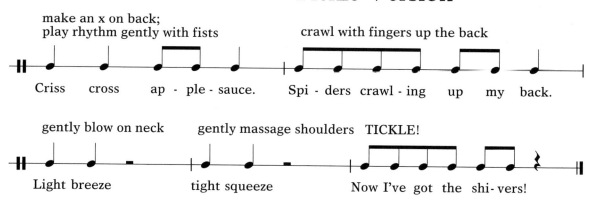

**Variations**

◆ Play in a circle with all facing the same direction, performing actions on the back of the person in front. Turn around and switch. (If anyone played the rhythms too hard, this is the moment for revenge!)

◆ Play in jazz style, adjusting the "light breeze ** tight squeeze **" to fit in one measure (speak as 8th notes). Play while listening to the recording *Blue Bubbles* from Don Byron's Bug Music, matching the dynamics and energy of the music. Choreograph variations—motions in the air, with partner, sitting, standing, moving freely to find new partner, etc.

The piece lasts for 3 minutes and 24 seconds, so have a few ideas up your sleeve—and marvel at how it all fits together, as if the piece were composed for this rhyme.

# Days of the Week

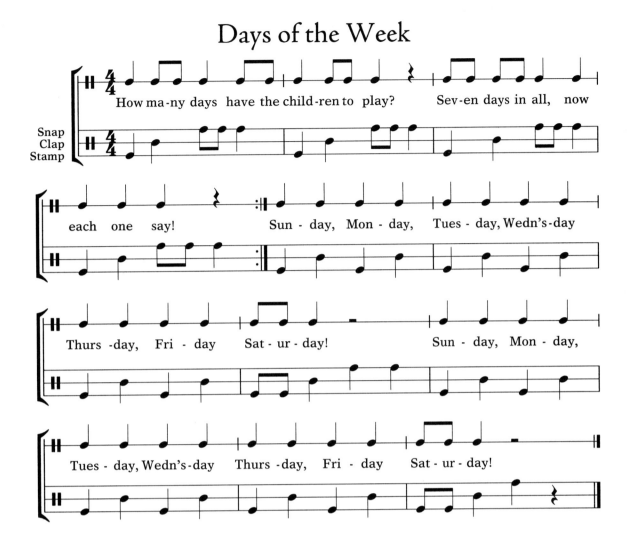

## 5. DAYS OF THE WEEK: The list, calendar controversy, foreign language study and a cultural thermometer

From phoneme to syllable to word, we arrive at the list—what better place to start than the days of the week? Kids in classrooms everywhere are already chanting the days—why not take the idea further and create a full-blown performance? Beginning with a variation of the Mother Goose rhyme *"How many days has my baby to play?"* we take a trip through complementary rhythms, offbeat claps, calendar controversies, commonalities amongst diverse languages and revelation about what our kids actually do with their free time.

### Teaching Suggestions
- Begin with accompanying rhythm and teach text echo fashion while continuing the rhythm.
- Let students recite the days and note whether they start on Sunday or Monday. Discuss their reasoning. (Sunday because that's what the calendar looks like. Monday because Sunday is considered the weekend, which naturally should be at the *end* of the week. And according to one story, the last day of the world's creation was a day of rest.)
- Give the music-teacher reason for starting on Monday—the closing rhythm of "Sa-tur-day" brings the phrase to a satisfying cadence.

- What is the relationship between the text and the clapping pattern? The clap always lands on "-day." Use this pattern to teach offbeat clapping. In the Language Extensions, we will see how this pattern re-occurs in different forms in other languages.

## Variations

- After reciting the rhyme and days as shown above, half group claps the rhythm of the opening rhyme ("How many days…") while the other half plays the accompaniment.
- Divide into seven groups, one for each day. Perform as above, with each day in turn miming activities they enjoy on that day while others clap the rhythms.
- Each group discusses its activities and briefly plans how to dramatize them through movement and mime. Play recorded music (*Sleigh Ride* from Don Byron's Bug Music a great choice), inviting each group one by one into the center (timed with the sections of the piece). At the end, all return for the grand finale and freeze.

## Language Extensions

This activity has been perfect for my international teaching, both allowing me to get under the skin of a language through learning the days of the week and providing different rhythms, structures and tonal color to the activity. Begin by asking your students if they know how to say the days in another language and let them be the teachers.

Many of the examples below follow the model of the repeated word. Some are at the end, some at the beginning and some have no repetition. Both the repeated patterns and breaks of that pattern will suggest the body percussion accordingly. For example, German uses "tag" (day) except for "Mittwoch" (mid-week). Thus, accompany with pat-clap, but change to pat-stamp on "Mittwoch." The Spanish re-occurring syllable is "-es," but the pattern is broken on "Sabado, Domingo," which can be snapped or stamped. The Mandarin version has the repeated words at the beginning (literally Day 1, Day 2, Day 3, etc.) with a variant for Sunday. With the children, make up matching body percussion parts in the language of your choice.

The following list represents just a fraction of the world's languages. I chose them because they are from countries where I have done this activity. For correct phonetic pronunciations below, I urge you to seek a native speaker in your school, neighborhood or local restaurant. Except for the Persian week, which begins on Saturday, all the examples below start with Monday, something I found universally true outside of the U.S.

- **Vietnamese:** thứr hai/ thứr ba/ thứr tur/ thứr nam/ thứr sáu/ thứr bay/ chu nhat
- **Mandarin:** Xingqi yi, Xingqi èr, Xingqi san, Xingqi si, Xingqi wu, Xingqi liu, Xingqi tian
- **Taiwanese:** Pai it, Pai ji, Pai sa, Pai si, Pai go, Pai lak, le Pai jit
- **Thai:** wan chan, wan angkan, wan phut, wan paruhat,[*] wan suk, wan sao, wan a-tit
- **Swahili:** jumatatu, jumanne, jumatano, alhamisi, ijumaa, jumamosi, jumapili
- **Ewe (Ghana):** Dzoda, Blada, Kuda, Yawoda, Fida, Memleda, Kosida
- **Turkish:** Pazartesi, Salı, Çarsamba, Persembe, Cuma, Cumartesi, Pazar
- **Persian:** doshanbeh, seshanbeh, chaharshanbeh, panjshanbeh, jom'e, shanbeh, yekshanbeh
- **Italian:** lunedì, martedì, mercoledì, giovedì, venerdì, sabato, domenica
- **Spanish:** lunes, martes, miércoles, jueves, viernes, sábado, domingo
- **German:** Montag, Dienstag, Mittwoch, Donnerstag, Freitag, Samstag, Sonnstag

For quick reference of other languages and the origins of the English days of the week, see www. Omniglot.com/language/phrases/days.php

---

[*] The full version is "wan parhuhat sobbordee," which makes for an interesting rhythmic break.

## 6. STATIONS: Alliteration, phrase and the perfect rainy-day class

This game was another gift from P.E. teacher Rudy Benton (see *Criss Cross Applesauce*). I learned it from him back in 1975 and it has been a favorite with my students for over three decades. When it has been raining for five days straight, when you're in-between units, when your creative planning juices have run dry or when you want to animate words in yet another way, *Stations* is the game for you! Good for kids from 3 to 93, great for social mixing (try it at your next party) and just plain unadulterated fun, *Stations* will enliven any music or language arts class. There are many preparatory steps to be taken at your own pace. Below is a sample sequence:

### Preparation
+ On mounted paper or cardboard, write the following:

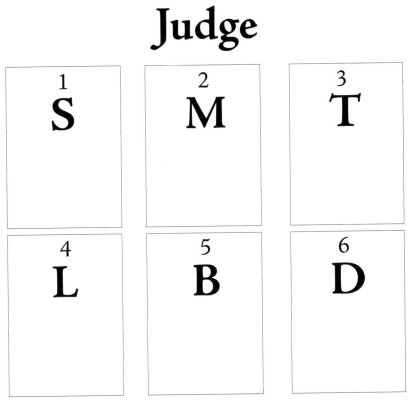

+ Show "S" and ask students to think of a word beginning with that letter (most of the little ones will say "snake") and then act out that word to musical accompaniment. Write a list on the board of other words: skip, slide, snail, soup, etc. and have kids mime each one.
+ Show "M" and write suggested words on the board. Ask for two words—an adjective and a noun (musical monkey) or an adverb and a verb (merrily mashing). Students mime. Combine the two (a musical monkey merrily mashing).
+ Show "T"—partners combine parts of speech (see above) and motions to make one tableau. (For example, in "Tina Turner teaching Tai Chi to a Turtle," one student is Tina and the other is a turtle.)
+ Show "L" —students brainstorm a series of words in groups of 3. (In "licking a lollipop languidly while listening to love songs," one might be the lollipop, the other the licker and the other miming the love song.
+ For a large class, continue as above with "B" and "D" with groups of 4 or 5.

**The Game**

- Put the cards on stools spread out throughout the room, with chairs in the front for the group called "Judges." Each group is assigned to one of the "stations." Each group quickly brainstorms their words and how they might do them (one minute or less to discuss and decide).
- When the teacher plays music (recorded or live), all stations mime their words. Moving around the room, the judges watch.
- After one or two minutes of music, all sit down at their station while the teacher interviews each judge. Each judge in turn chooses a group that he or she liked and the group tells (not shows) what the words were.
- After all judges have named their favorite, the remaining groups tell their words.
- All switch and move to the next numbered station (Judges go to 1, last station goes to Judge). The groups remain together throughout the class.
- Repeat above process; short brainstorm and discussion, show when new music comes on, sit down when music ends, judges choose, groups share, all move on.

**Criteria**

What are the judges looking for?

1) **An intriguing idea.** While the little ones will simply be snakes, the 3rd graders enjoy stringing as many words together as they can, like "a silly snake stirring and sipping samosa soup while dancing salsa to Santana."

2) **Interesting blend of bodies.** Again, the little ones tend to start with each being a snake or sipping soup, but when they join to all make one long snake or one is the soup bowl, one the spoon and one the sipper, the results are more interesting.

3) **Coherent and graceful execution.** The old jazz adage "'taint what you do, but the way that you do it" applies here. Sharp focus, levels, clear movements and interesting shapes will always impress the judges.

4) **Attention to the quality of the music.** Groups that can adapt their ideas to different musical styles, fitting their motions to a waltz, a gentle bossa nova or an explosive James Brown tune, will likely attract the judges' attention. Sometimes I announce the next music and sometimes I catch them by surprise. Here's your chance to expose your students to the music that you love.

**Stations** improves over time, from one class to the next, from the first time to the 15th. Within each class, it takes time for the kids to warm up, but once the ideas are in the air, the sparks start to fly and the excitement is palpable. Besides the pure fun, the lessons are many: alliteration, social cooperation, movement expression, creating coherent phrases and intriguing images matching movement with the music… the list goes on. All of which makes this the perfect game for a rainy day—or any day.

# I Saw Esau–Rondo

**Part One**

I saw E-sau sit-ting on a see-saw, E-sau, he saw me

Clap

**Part Two**

I saw E-sau sit-ting on a see-saw, E-sau, he saw me.

Snap
Clap
Pat

**Part Three**

I saw E-sau sit-ting on a see-saw, E-sau, he saw me.

Snap
Clap
Pat

**B Section**

Snap
Clap
Pat

E - sau see-saw see-saw E - sau E - sau see-saw see-saw see.

**C Section**

I saw E - sau kis-sing Kate. The fact is we all three saw. For

I saw him and he saw me, and she saw I saw E - sau.

FORM: part one/ B section/ Parts one and two/ C section/ Parts one, two, three / All parts at once

### 7. I SAW ESAU: Alliteration, assonance, the sentence and a Bible story

This delightful tongue twister is a veritable playground of poetic devices—alliteration (all those "s" sounds) assonance (all those "e" sounds), homophones ("-sau, saw")* and homonyms ("I *saw*, see-*saw*)." In this arrangement, we teeter and totter through both the linguistic and musical possibilities, with a Biblical reference and spying on young lovers thrown into the mix. Especially delightful is the feeling of see-sawing alone, the voice going up while the hands go down.

### Teaching Process
- Begin by speaking the text and clapping on all the "sau/saw" sounds.
- Speak in low, middle, high voice, parallel with the body percussion in part three.
- As above, parallel with the body percussion in part two. Repeat with contrary motion.
- Divide group in three, each on one part of the score. Repeat speaking instead of singing.
- Practice B and C section.
- Orchestrate, following suggested form.

### Variations
- Choose some parts of the score rather than teaching the whole thing.
- Partners recite the poem hocket style, alternating words while seesawing opposite each other. Whoever lands on the first clap after "me" takes a shape; partner immediately copies it. Repeat with other partner beginning.
- Transfer body percussion to small percussion instruments.

### Extensions
- Tell the story of Esau from the Bible. (Genesis 25–19–29)

  Esau and Jacob were twins born to Isaac and Rebekkah. Esau, born first, was a hunter and favored by Isaac, while Jacob was more domestic and favored by Rebekkah. One day Esau came home empty-handed from the hunt and asked Jacob for some of the soup he had made. Jacob offered it to him on the condition that he give up his birthright as the elder son. Hungry and short-sighted, Esau sold his birthright for a bowl of soup.

---

* Quick grammar review: Homophones are two words pronounced alike but spelled differently with different meanings (rose, rows) and homonyms are two words pronounced and spelled alike with different meanings (rose-the flower, rose-the verb/ rows the boat, rows of roses).

# Hannah Bantry

FORM: Layer ostinati to accompany text. Choose different combinations (voices 2 and 4/ 2 and 3/ 3 and 4) to accompany.

### 8. HANNAH BANTRY: More assonance, consonance, the nursery rhyme and secret hungers

Hannah appeals to our secret hungers and the children are delighted to imagine her hidden in the pantry chewing away so greedily, with no manners whatsoever. The vocal ostinati, drawn from the vowels and consonants of the text, are intended to evoke the sounds of her chewing.

When recording this song with the 1st graders many years back, I had a brilliant idea—record them reciting the text clearly the first time and the second time while chewing on bread. What was meant to give the feeling of Hanna greedily gnawing away in the pantry simply sounded like a bunch of kids with very poor annunciation—a sonic disaster! After a good laugh, we quickly shelved the idea.

Hannah Bantry joins her fellow nursery rhyme characters Charley Barley, Humpty Dumpty, Georgie Porgie and Jack Sprat as one of the rhymed (and slant-rhymed) names that tickle our ear so.

### Extension

- Invite the students to give themselves a rhymed nickname (Dougie Wuggie).
- Extend the name into the first line of a rhyme: (Dougie Wuggie drove a buggy…)

# Moses Supposes

Body Percussion

Clap
Chest
Pat Thighs
Back of Thighs
Step

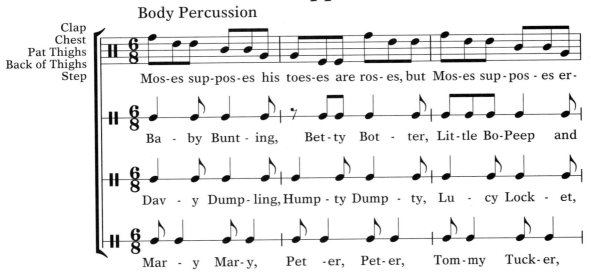

Mos-es sup-pos-es his toes-es are ros-es, but Mos-es sup-pos-es er-

Ba - by Bunt - ing,   Bet-ty Bot - ter,   Lit-tle Bo-Peep   and

Dav - y Dump-ling, Hump-ty Dump - ty,   Lu - cy Lock - et,

Mar - y Mar-y,   Pet - er,   Pet-er,   Tom-my Tuck-er,

ro - ne-ous-ly.   For no-bod-ies toes-es are po-sies of ros-es as

Lit - tle Boy Blue.   Goose - y Gan - der, Greg-or-y Griggs,

Char - lie Wag.   Lit - tle Miss Muf   fet, Sim - ple Sim - on,

Tom   the pi-per's son Mar - y Mar - y,   Pet - er,   Pet - er,

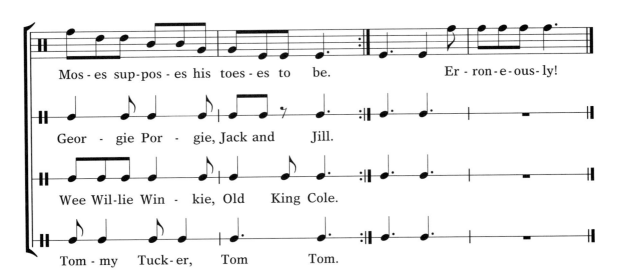

Mos - es sup-pos - es his toes - es to   be.      Er - ron-e-ous-ly!

Geor - gie Por - gie, Jack and   Jill.

Wee Wil-lie Win - kie, Old   King Cole.

Tom - my Tuck - er,   Tom     Tom.

### 9. MOSES SUPPOSES: Ostinato, rhyme and a playground of sonic devices

This speech piece began by making a list of alliterative and rhymed nursery rhyme characters. When I'm standing on my soap-box lamenting how nursery rhymes have been washed away in the tsunami of media-ocrity, pop culture, too-busy parents and video games, I often note what a great loss it is for children never to meet this colorful cast of characters, never to taste on their tongue the flavor of Betty Botter's butter or Peter Piper's peppers. While scrolling through the alphabet trying to prove my point, I hit upon the idea of putting them all into one speech piece. When it became clear that a piece built solely on ostinati wasn't enough, *Moses Supposes* seemed the perfect rhyme for a melodic layer.

Here is our first piece in 6/8, the preferred meter of Mother Goose. You may note that many of the arrangements in the next section shift the natural 6/8 meter to 2/4 or 4/4. The pedagogical reasons for this will be made clear later.

With all the ostinati, this arrangement is quite dense—so feel free to try other combinations. And don't forget to show the kids what Gene Kelly and Donald O'Connor do with this rhyme in the film *Singing in the Rain*.

### Extensions

While working on this rhyme, I happened to be reading "Nicholas Nickleby." Nicholas had just met Newman Noggs and it gave me the idea of scanning through the long list of Dickens characters to see how he used alliteration, rhyme, rhythm and more to create memorable names for his characters. The result is included here and again, the texture is quite dense, so thin it out as needed. For a "melody," try reading freely the opening of *A Tale of Two Cities*: "It was the best of times. It was the worst of times…"

# Dickens Characters

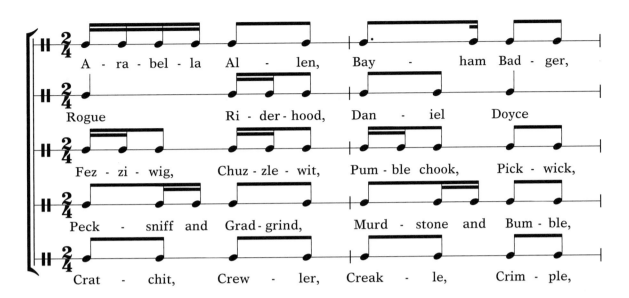

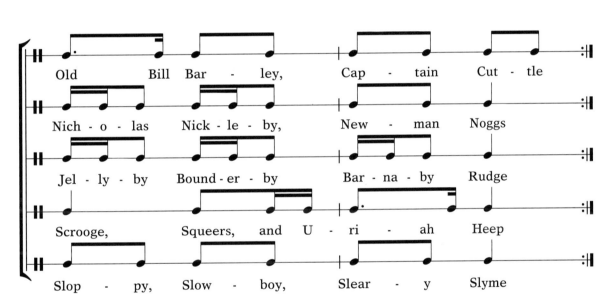

# Ecuador Speech Piece

**TRANSLATION:** *Latacunga, Jipijapa, Riobamba, Chugchilan, Cuenca, Guayaquil, Baños, Quito* are all cities in Ecuador. *Las Islas del Galápagos*—Galápagos Islands. *Ceviche*—marinated raw fish. *Salchipapa*—a potato and sausage dish. *Patacones*—fried plantain. *Queso*—cheese. *Pan*—bread. *Montañas*—mountains. *Selva*—jungle. *Playa*—beach. *Estas son las maravillas del país Ecuador*—These are the wonders of the country Ecuador.

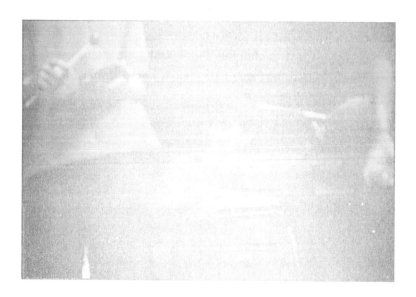

## 10. ECUADOR SPEECH PIECE: Speech to percussion, food and geography

While on a four-hour bus ride in Ecuador, I was looking at the map and noticing the musicality of the city names. And as we stopped at each place, I found myself enjoying the musical calls of the food vendors as much as the food. So while bouncing up and down on the bumpy mountain roads, I set to work on a speech piece and this is the result.

The piece makes no attempt to duplicate traditional Ecuadorian music, but draws from the music of the speech. It also celebrates this marvelous country, its mountains, jungles and beaches all side by side—and its delicious food. This is best reserved for the older kids (I used it with 6th grade), as the rhythmic texture is dense and highly syncopated. The three-part form is as follows:

**PART 1:** Write down the city names on file cards. Small groups (two to five) select a card and work on making a rhythmic ostinato, spoken or sung, with gesture or dance.

One group is "tourists" walking through the bus station. Each group tries to entice the tourists onto their "bus" as they walk by them. First time passing through, the first group fades out as the tourists arrive at second group, second stops when they arrive at the third, and so on. At the end, the tourists recite the whole rhyme. They pass the groups again, this time all adding on. At end, all recite the rhyme while walking to the instruments.

**PART 2:** Layer the percussion parts one at a time. When all parts are in, one group recites rhyme. (This may need to be amplified or percussionists can play softer.)

**PART 3:** Percussionists all play light beat while select drums "trade 8's" (improvise for 8 beats each) back and forth. At cue, re-enter with all parts, recite rhyme once more and end.

## 11. ENGINE ENGINE NUMBER NINE: Compositional devices for creating texture, intrapersonal intelligence

> Engine engine number nine,
> Going down Chicago line.
> If the train stops on the track,
> Do you want your money back?
> Yes. No. Maybe so!
> Yes. No. Maybe so!

This charming counting-out rhyme is fertile ground for the Orff class imagination. I've done some fifteen variations and then watched my colleagues Sofía López-Ibor and James Harding take the children on their own marvelous rides through the countryside. (Indeed, the whole subject of trains in music and movement is so rich that it deserves a book in itself—keep your eye out for some future collection from Sofía, James and myself.)

Meanwhile, I use it here to give examples of five basic orchestral devices used frequently in Orff classes. They are wonderful tools to extend any rhyme, develop listening and ensemble skills and initiate children into some elemental compositional techniques that create instantly satisfying and workable textures. Let's examine them one by one:

**CANON:** This simple device, as old as medieval England and wide as the Ituri Rainforest in Africa, is a staple of the Orff classroom. Also called a "round," a canon repeats the same material with voices entering at different places. There are body percussion canons, movement canons, speech canons and the more common melodic canons (like *Frere Jacques*). Whereas melodic canons are restricted by harmonic considerations, speech canons will almost always work. Following the say, play, say and play model, you can instantly create body percussion canons as well. The example given below begins as a two-part canon with the entrance after two beats, followed by a four-part canon with the entrance after one beat.

# Engine Engine—Canon

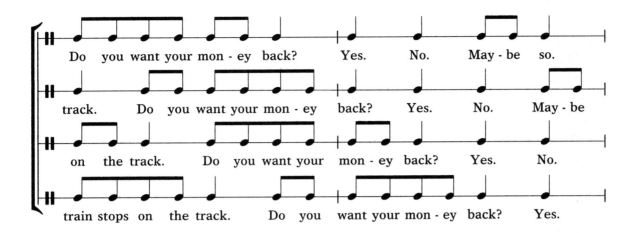

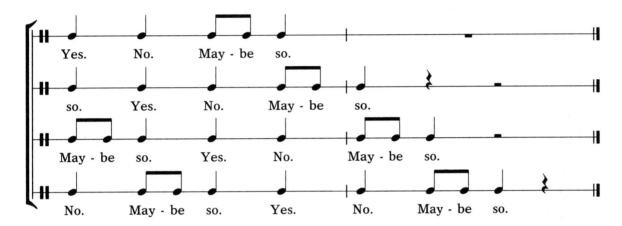

**OSTINATO:** We've already explored how to accompany text with many kinds of ostinati: vocal percussion, additional text, movement and body percussion. Here I introduce Keith Terry's* work that uses four phrases of 3, 5, 7 and 9. The example given here uses them in their original form; for a more interesting variation that lends itself to some simple movement, try the following:

3—Play three sets of 3 and take 2 quarter note steps.
5—The "new five" is "clap pat pat step step"
7—The "new seven" is "clap chest chest pat pat step step"
9—Remains the same.

Since all of the above now include the feet, each group moves on the steps. In a circle facing right (with the group divided into quadrants), this gives the effect of each group "pushing" the other forward a bit as the train circles around. Perform as shown once or twice through the text and then reverse direction, with a "pulling" effect. Last time, face center and move toward center.

This particular arrangement is composed of simple parts that create a quite complex effect—save it for the older kids.

---

* Keith Terry is a performing musician and recording artist whose work includes two instructional DVD's on his groundbreaking approach to body percussion. (www.crosspulse.com)

# Engine Engine Number Nine

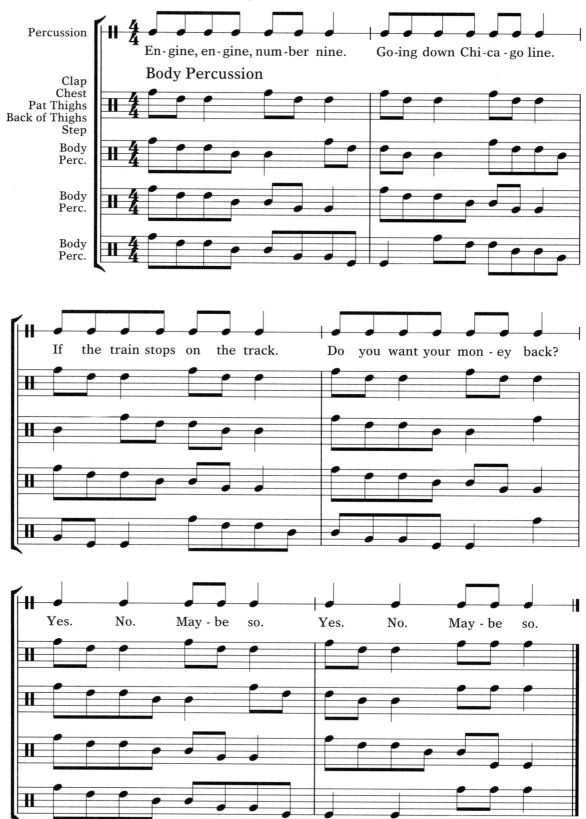

Percussion

En-gine, en-gine, num-ber nine.    Go-ing down Chi-ca-go line.

Clap
Chest
Pat Thighs
Back of Thighs
Step

## Body Percussion

Body Perc.

Body Perc.

Body Perc.

If the train stops on the track.    Do you want your mon-ey back?

Yes.    No.    May-be so.    Yes.    No.    May-be so.

**HOCKET:** *The Harvard Dictionary of Music* defines hocket thus:

> "In polyphony of the 13th and 14th centuries, a stylistic device or a self-contained composition characterized by the distribution of a melodic line between two voices in such a way that as one sounds the other is silent."

It goes on to say,

> "…although the genre is often mentioned by the theorists, only eleven examples are known to survive."

Though it does acknowledge that "texture of this type is prominent in the music of some non-Western cultures and is especially characteristic of some African music," it fails to give any concrete examples. Hocket is a universal principle, found throughout Africa in Pygmy vocal music, Ugandan amadinda xylophone music, Ghanaian por-por taxi driver-horn music, various Balinese gamelan compositions, Thai ankglung ensembles, Peruvian panpipe music, handbell choirs and various Western contemporary compositions. Hocket is less common in Orff classrooms than the other devices shown here, but is a marvelous tool for exercising the musical brain and creating an intriguing texture.

How does hocket work in speech pieces? Each person in turn says one word, syllable or beat of a text in the order they appear. The example below uses one beat, with the exception of the final "maybe so." This starts off simply enough, but is challenging when a word is divided across a beat, as in *Down Chi-cago*. Each of the numbers below indicate one speaker, the underlined word or words, one beat. Naturally, if the group is smaller than 22 people, the chant will keep circulating around.

| | | | |
|---|---|---|---|
| 1. Engine | 2. engine | 3. number | 4. nine |
| 5. Going | 6. down Chi– | 7. cago | 8. line |
| 9. If the | 10. train stops | 11. on the | 12. track |
| 13. Do you | 14. want your | 15. money | 16. back? |
| 17. Yes. | 18. No. | 19. Maybe | so. |
| 20. Yes. | 21. No. | 22. Maybe | so. |

This takes some practice. Start with slow tempo and gradually increase the speed. Once the children are comfortable, the fun begins.

- All pat beat while the text is spoken as above.
- The one who gets the first "Yes" (17) has to make a large gesture while speaking the word, "No" (18) makes a different gesture and "Maybe so" (19), yet a different gesture. Numbers 20, 21 and 22 not only have to say their words on time, but copy the gestures (20 copies 17, 21 copies 18, 22 copies 19).

I always tell the students that everything we learn is for the pleasure of learning and music class is not about dividing the group into "winners and losers." That said and done, the game gets a lot more exciting and the children really perk up when we play the above as a winning game. Whoever forgets to say their word, says the wrong word, or misses the beat is out. If you forget to make a gesture on "yes," "no" or "maybe so" or don't copy the gesture correctly, you're also out. Game resumes starting with the next person, so it's always a surprise to those who get the gesture words.

These games weed out the kids who are less accomplished and it may seem like cruel and unusual punishment that those who need the practice most don't get it. Three solutions:

1) Sometimes kids learn more away from the pressure, sitting outside the game and watching.
2) After a certain number of kids get out, they form their own circle, playing at the same time, but with no one going out.

3) Kids out choose a percussion instrument and which word of the text to play. When all are out, playing the game again with percussion instruments produces a random, but coherent, orchestration.

In short, everyone wins.

**AUGMENT/ DIMINISH:** You may remember this concept from your study of Bach fugues, though once again, it is a universal principle, common in Javanese and Balinese gamelan music. The basic idea is to play a theme (or speak a text) at half (augmentation) or double (diminution) the normal speed. This is especially relevant to our train theme, as it creates a feeling of three trains going different speeds, but all arriving at the station simultaneously.

This is a good place to include a variation (co-composed with my daughter, Talia Goodkin) that can be used to divide into groups.

> Engine Engine Number Nine
> Is your engine running fine?
> Is it high or is it low?
> Tell me now so I will know.
> High. Low. (clap) Just so! (2x)

This came from a question Talia and her co-teacher would ask their second graders, "How is your engine running today?" (The perfect metaphor for their two students obsessed with cars.) This is an excellent exercise for learning how to turn inward and check your emotional state and energy level. What Howard Gardner calls the "intrapersonal intelligence" is a universal potential like all others that can grow smarter with practice. When children (and adults) can step back and name an emotion, they take the first step toward owning their feelings.

- After reciting the rhyme with a simple pat-clap, the first eight people in the circle answer with "high" or "low" or "just so." Repeat the rhyme at the end.
- Once all have answered, they join one of the following groups:

The "high" group which recites the diminished version, the "low" group which recites the augmented version or the "just so" group which recites the normal version.

For greater expression, speak the augmented text in a low, monster-like voice, the diminished text in a high, munchkin-like voice and the normal—well, normal.

**Variation**

An intriguing—and challenging—variation: One group starts off speaking the text slowly and accelerates like a train pulling out of the station. The other group begins at a fast tempo and gradually slows down, like a train pulling into the station. The challenge is for both groups to end at the same time. Be sure to introduce the formal music terms for gradually getting faster (*accelerando*) or slower (*ritardando*).

# Engine Engine–Augment/Diminish

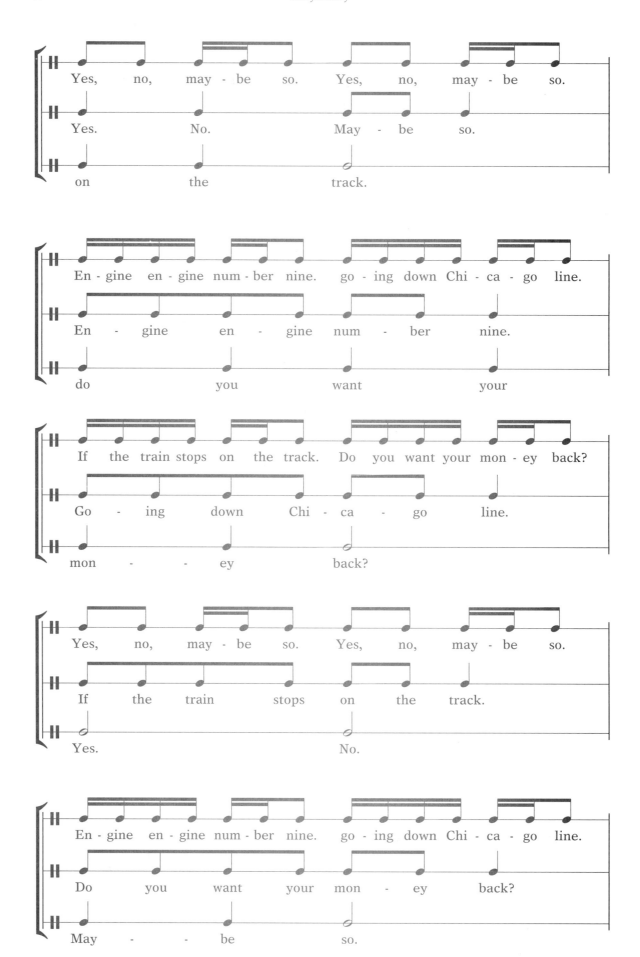

**RONDO:** The rondo is a musical form that satisfies our need for repetition and variation. It begins with an opening statement (A), goes off to a b section and returns to the familiar A, only to take off again in a new direction with C. And so it continues—ABACAD—for as long as we have new places to go. Below is a possible rondo form for this rhyme.

- A section: Perform hand jive with a partner (pat knees, clap, pat partner's hands, clap) while reciting text.
- B section: Walk around the room attached as a two-car train, improvising chugging and whistling sounds. Internalize the length of the rhyme (24 beats) while walking.
- A section: Clap again with partner.
- C section: Immediately join two other partners to make a four-person train.
- A section: Perform hand jive in group of four.
- D section: An eight-person train. Continue until all are in one long train.

The variations of the B, C, D, etc. sections are the length of the trains. But for added interest, suggest various scenarios just before the train pulls out: up a steep mountain, on a curvy track, backing up, going through a tunnel (with two eight-car trains, one can form the tunnel and then switch).

**Variations—other possibilities for B, C, D, etc. sections**
- Recite other poems or sing songs about trains between each A section.
- Improvise body percussion.
- Play (one at a time) melodies composed to the text on the xylophones.

**REVIEW:** Canon, ostinato and rondo are the music teacher's friends and the student's delight. Hocket and augment/diminish, while less commonly used, are equally effective in creating complex music from a simple text. Consider exploring one of the above with each class and performing them in combination as an extended work. Remember these principles in subsequent texts and invite the students to use them in their own compositions. When your teaching feels tired and worn, when your "train gets stuck on the track," these ideas are just the ticket to get you going again!

### 12. BOW WOW WOW (speech): Beat, Rhythm, Color, Ostinato—an introduction to elemental orchestration

"Let the children be their own composers," said Carl Orff, capturing in a mere seven words a radically different approach to music education. He began with a vision of tapping children's creative potential from the very beginning of their formal schooling and then proceeded to give the details as to how that might work. This lesson introduces four elemental principles—beat, rhythm, color, ostinato— that guide children toward coherent composition and understanding. This sequence is particularly relevant for the 5 to 7 year old children, but works with beginning music students of any age. The suggested order is flexible.

#### 1) BEAT
* Pat the beat while saying text.
* Explore a variety of ways to play the beat—pat, snap, clap, click tongue, walk, hammer, saw, text message, etc.
* Alone, with partners, or in small groups, students find their own way to express beat.
* Define beat: *The steady underlying pulsation inside the music.* A foundation for music-making, like rice in a meal.

#### 2) RHYTHM
* Clap the rhythm of the words while saying them; while thinking them.
* Explore ways to play the rhythm (as above—patting, snapping, etc.)
* Alone, with partners or in small groups, students find their own way to express the rhythm. This might include combinations of patting, clapping, etc.
* In half groups or partners, one plays the beat, the other the rhythm. Switch.
* Define rhythm: *A combination of short and long sounds and rests grouped into phrases.* The way the words go. The vegetables and meat that go over the rice.

#### 3) COLOR
* Listen for the rests in the text and fill with a snap.
* Find other ways to express color.
* Groups of three create expressions of beat, rhythm and color. Switch.
* Define color: *A sound or gesture that fills in the rests or accents key parts of the rhythm.* Gives a splash of color. The spices in the rice dish.

#### 4) OSTINATO
* Clap a short repeated rhythmic pattern that complements the text. Students play ostinato while reciting the text.
* As above, with a combination of pats, claps, stamps or snaps.
* Students create their ostinati.
* Groups of four create a mini-composition, choosing how to express beat, rhythm, color, and ostinato. Switch so everyone plays all parts.
* Perform.
* Define ostinato: *A short, repeated pattern.* It complements the rhythms in the text, adds flavor and texture, like peanuts in our rice dish.

Turning the creative choices over to the students will yield fun and surprising results—like a composition based on dog sounds or keeping the beat by wiggling your ears. Below is a more systematic approach, taking this process through different levels of body percussion.

# Bow Wow Wow—Pat/clap

# Bow Wow Wow—Clap/pat/stamp

**EXTENSIONS**

- Explore ways to play two at a time by yourself, e.g., pat beat with left hand, play rhythm with right hand or step beat, vocalize rhythm.
- Switch (rhythm in left hand, beat in right or vocalize beat, step rhythm).
- Play four at once, e.g., tap beat with foot, play rhythm with right hand, ostinato with left, click tongue for color part.
- Switch.

These systematic exercises work wonders in developing rhythmic proficiency. Expressing rhythm in different parts of the body and in different combinations anchors it firmly in the body, deepens understanding and enlarges the expressive vocabulary. And you can practice them anywhere—stuck in traffic, waiting for the dentist, taking a shower.

- Create composition as above with vowel sounds; consonants; animal sounds.
- Transfer all to unpitched percussion, one type of instrument for each musical element (drum, shaker, bell, woodblock). Switch parts (i.e., drums play beat, then rhythm, etc.).
- Create other text to accompany rhyme.

# Bow Wow Wow—Vocal

## SUMMARY

Why do children respond so enthusiastically to the sequence presented here?

- ⋆ They develop an understanding of basic concepts that empower them to think more clearly about music.
- ⋆ They develop their ensemble skills by playing each part in relation to another.
- ⋆ They experience creating at each level and get much-needed repetition through refreshing variation.
- ⋆ They learn a working vocabulary that will be useful for the rest of their music education (in future compositions, you might overhear them saying, "We need a good complementary ostinato here").
- ⋆ They exercise their social skills and enjoy the pleasure of creating something with their classmates.
- ⋆ They have a foundation that enables them to continue improvising and composing on the Orff instruments.

And that brings us into the next section of the book—orchestrations for the Orff ensemble.

6th graders performing on Orff instruments.

# PART II: ARRANGEMENTS FOR ORFF INSTRUMENTS

Beginning Arrangements—Kindergarten to 2nd Grade:
DO Pentatonic and Pentatonic Modes

**From Body to Instrument**

Tell people you teach music and they reply, "What instrument do you teach?" Naturally, mastering a musical instrument is an important part of music education, but music is much larger than that. Our first, and most important instruments, are our body and voice. As Section 1 demonstrates, we can make a great deal of expressive music through body percussion, vocalizing, chanting and singing. At all ages—witness Bobby McFerrin, Keith Terry, Acapella and Steppin' groups. These expressive mediums are perfect for beginning music education—accessible to all and available 24/7.

For the young child, the next step in expanding the expressive palette is to explore a variety of simple percussion instruments—shakers, scrapers, woodblocks, cowbells, hand drums and more. Played with the hand, a stick or a mallet, the instrumental technique is prepared through body percussion and the rhythms prepared from the rhymes (see the piece *Ecuador* for a good example of this). As I have written of these possibilities in my book *Sound Ideas*, we won't go into much detail here. Instead, we will see how to orchestrate these rhymes and poems for the Orff instrument ensemble.

**The Orff Instruments**

The Orff instruments were first developed by Carl Orff in the late 1920's in his work with young adult dancers in an experimental school in Munich, Germany. He and his colleague Gunild Keetman later used them with children in the 1950's and they now can be found in music classrooms from South Africa to north Finland, from Korea to Kansas. The instruments are designed as a child-sized orchestra, complete with a range from C below middle C (now also an octave below with the addition of contra-bass bars) to A almost four octaves higher. The three instrument types— xylophone, metallophone and glockenspiel—produce distinct timbres that give color to orchestration. The genius of these instruments is their clean musical tone produced with minimal technique, their removable bars that allow children to play scales with no "wrong notes" and their adaptability within any arrangement, as bass, chords and melodies can all be practiced on any instrument.

The first function of the Orff instruments is to accompany the voice. In these arrangements, we will grow familiar with the musical devices that the children use to accompany their own speaking and singing. The children also learn to play the melodies they sing and most importantly, invent melodies themselves. Here is where the nursery rhyme is the perfect vehicle for improvisation and composition.

The text provides both the rhythm and the phrasing for melodic invention. Because most rhymes have no set melody,* they free the child (and the teacher) to compose or improvise one. Some rhymes, of course, have been inextricably linked with popular melodies—*Twinkle Little Star, Mary Had a Little Lamb, This Old Man,* etc.—and though I sing these with the children, I rarely play them on the Orff instruments. Virtually all of the melodies in this book are pentatonic (the above are not) accompanied by a drone and were either created by the children or me and often, by a combination of both.

The arrangements in this section follow our first and second grade curriculum, highlighting the following basic concepts:

- **Rhythm:** quarter/ eighth/ quarter rest; 2/4–4/4
- **Melody:** Sol–mi songs, sol–mi–la, Do pentatonic in key of C, Re and La mode in C
- **Harmony:** Simple drone (C and G played together), broken drone (alternating C and G), level drone (C and G played low, then an octave higher), crossover drone (C–G–C$^1$)
- **Texture:** Rhythmic and melodic ostinato, color part
- **Form:** ABA, Rondo, Canon

Keep in mind that the Orff ensemble experience is just one part of a larger program that includes games, movement studies, folk dances, songs, notational exercises and more, some of which is, and all of which can be, integrated into the arrangements given.

4th graders playing Orff instruments

---

* J.W. Eliott, an English composer from the Victorian Era, composed many melodies to nursery rhymes, all in a diatonic harmonic style not appropriate for use by young children on Orff instruments.

# Rain Rain

Begin adding one voice at a time. Perform rondo style, each instrumental group improvising eight-bar melodies in C pentatonic scale. End with *diminuendo* before final note.

## 13. RAIN, RAIN: Beginning orchestration for Orff Ensemble and puddle splashing

*Rain, Rain* is the perfect song for getting your feet wet in the Orff orchestra. I use the following sequence to introduce the Orff instruments at my teacher workshops and it never fails to initiate everyone into the world of musical magic. (I always end by saying, "Welcome to first grade.") We will go into great detail in this first piece in order to illuminate key concepts implied in all pieces to follow.

### Process of development

- All seated at the Orff instruments facing the teacher. Instruments are grouped by range (bass, alto, soprano) and timbre (xylophone, metallophone, glockenspiel). Teacher's alto xylophone is backwards (low bars on right) so that students can mirror left-right motion. The story begins:

  It was a rainy day in _____ (your location) and all the children were getting restless. The rain just would not stop.

- Following teacher, all simulate raindrops on the low C bar of the instrument with fingertips. Teacher moves to D and all follow, to E, etc.

  The rain fell so hard that some branches in the trees fell and had to be removed.

- Move to F and then remove that bar. Continue playing G, A, then remove B, following the story above. Then high C, D, E, remove F, then G and A. If the xylophone ends there (some continue) play on the wood at the end of the instrument. At the end of this process, the xylophone will be set up in a C pentatonic scale:

      C D E  G A  C D E  G A

- Run backs of fingers up and down the bars, creating a glissando effect.

  The children tried their magic chant to see if the rain would go away.

- All whisper and freely speak (no set beat or meter) the text while playing bars as above.

  But the rain kept falling.

- Tremolo on low C again with both hands using fingers. Continue C with left hand and move right hand to D, then E, G. Play C and G together to a beat and sing text twice.

  The rain didn't stop, but it fell a little differently.

- Alternate C and G. Sing song again (always twice).

  And then again differently.

- C, G, high C, G. Sing on vocable "loo."

  And yet again.

- Low C and G. High C and G. Sing with solfege. (Sol mi sol-sol mi....)

  The rain just kept falling, but it fell differently on different buildings.

- All choose their own version of drones outlined above, including creating new variations. Sing text again.

  After a while, the rain stopped in some parts of town and you could only hear it on the biggest buildings downtown.

- Basses continue playing their chosen drones with their fingers.

  Then in mid-town, it started raining again. The people put up their umbrellas.

- Alto xylophones copy teacher with right pointer finger in air like an umbrella and left hand playing ostinato "C–D–E–D" in quarter notes.

  They got under an overhang and heard the rain falling even faster.

- Right hand alternates on G, creating an 8th note ostinato (C–G–D–G–E–G–D–G- etc.). Continue traveling through the "neighborhoods," adding the parts shown in the score one group at a time. Sing the song twice when all parts are in.

  Well, the song just didn't seem to be working because now it was raining harder.

- Basses pick up mallets and resume drones. Continue group by group. Check balance while singing song (it should be quiet enough to hear the song).

  Well, now the children were really getting restless. One looked out the window and thought it might be fun to skip through the puddles. She knew her parents would be mad, so while they were busy talking on their cell phones, she snuck out the door and splashed in a puddle. But she didn't stay out too long and got home before her parents finished talking.

- Teacher improvises on all five notes of the pentatonic scale for 16 beats and ends on C.

  When the other children saw her, they wanted to go play too. Soon, a whole group went out to play, but made sure they got home in time!

- All alto xylophones improvise, then sopranos, then metallophones, then glockenspiels.

  When the grown-ups saw how much fun the kids were having, they decided to go out too.

- All basses improvise.

  But they didn't know how to play like children.

  (This is one way to show that lower instruments generally don't improvise under the higher ones.)

  They all sang the song again and gradually, it seemed like it was raining less.

- All parts get quieter. Switch back to fingers without losing momentum. Return to tremolo on C, on C–D, C–E, C–G, C–A, C–C1. Stay on octave C's.

  And they lived happily ever after.

  (All play octave C in unison)

  Leave a dramatic moment of silence, pick up mallets again and tap them together for quiet applause.

### The Power and Purpose of Music

If all has gone well, the players will feel the satisfaction of leaving "clock time" and entering a world of great beauty. They will experience the magic of making the first tentative raindrop of sound out of silence, following it through its many changes and letting it ease back into silence. They will have touched the essence of music's power and purpose.

Life's great rhythms, from the microcosm of each breath to the grand arch of life from womb to tomb, all tend toward this cycle of beginning, middle, end. We awaken in the morning, go forth into the day and go to sleep at night. We are born, we live our life, we die. Music is both the experience and the metaphor for these rhythmic cycles.

But more importantly, it is the artful crafting of this cycle that gives a meaning, shape and beauty to it all. We may awake to the blast of the alarm, go through a day in which everything feels disconnected and far from beautiful, go to sleep with our anxieties joining us on the pillow. But in well-crafted music, the beginning is enticing, the middle connected, each note proceeding logically and inexorably to the next, and the ending satisfying. We may prefer some musical stories and styles over others, but even music that doesn't please our ears still holds true to this pattern.

*Rain Rain* enchants us because the parts develop logically, one leading to the other in ever-increasing texture. It comforts us with its familiar A section and keeps us alert with its variations. Like a rainstorm, it moves from the first drop to the last with all the excitement of the storm in-between. What's most remarkable is that it pleases adults and children alike. The parts are simple, but musical, and playable by just about any beginning music student without the sweat and tedium of hours of practice. And herein lies both the genius of the Orff instruments and the power of elemental composition. Enjoyable to all, accessible to all, playable by all—and exquisitely musical. We are all born with the seed of musical intelligence and *Rain Rain* is the perfect piece to water it. At any age.

**Process**

As lovely as this piece is, it needs another layer of understanding to communicate its full message. What makes this piece magical is as much the way we arrive at the notes as the notes themselves. It is not enough to teach a piece—*the process of teaching it must be musical*. Like a good piece of music, the class should begin with an enticing beginning and end with a satisfying ending. In between is a connected middle that never loses its flow, is never interrupted by verbal explanation. Instead, we use a story to stitch all the parts together, a story that evokes useful imagery ("coming home on time") and practical directions ("it only rained on the tall buildings"). Because we expect plot development in even the simplest of stories, the children are motivated to find out what happens next and listen with a different kind of attention.

People who attend Orff workshops are fascinated by this kind of attention to process. They experience its pleasure as they are led step by step into memorable musical experiences. But to turn around and do it yourself as a teacher is a whole other ballgame. Teachers in Orff trainings may experience hundreds of pitch-perfect lessons, but I know from my own experience coaching practice-teaching sessions that it is supremely difficult to change bad habits. And explaining too much at the expense of musical flow is one of the most common bad habits we teachers have.

Experiencing a model of seamless musical teaching helps us to mend our ways, but alone is often not enough—sometimes it is more helpful to watch a bad model and feel the contrast. Below is a scenario depicting how I might have taught this lesson before I knew better. Before it gets too far, I hope it finds you laughing. That means you're on the right track.

> "Okay, everyone quiet down. Today we're going to play a song called "Rain Rain" and you're going to learn four different kinds of drones—simple, broken, crossover and level. We'll also be learning about ostinato and sing a melody with a falling minor third. Who know how many half-steps that is? Okay, now basses, here's your part. Altos, stop playing! I'm working with the basses now. Discipline, discipline! Okay, next we're going to add the alto part. It goes like this..."

Get the idea? When you find yourself slipping into this kind of mode, stop, have a good laugh and then look at the following principles posted on your bulletin board.

- Keep the musical flow going without pause, with an enticing beginning, a connected middle and a satisfying ending.
- Proceed from simple to complex.
- Teach all the parts to everyone, then orchestrate.
- Enter through story instead of directions, images instead of rules.
- Adapt to the needs of your group and simplify parts as necessary.
- Move from imitation to creation, from given parts to improvisation.

*Rain Rain* is the foundation of all the pieces to come, both in its model of process and its elemental style of orchestration.

# Bluebells Cockleshells

Continue rondo form with two more vegetables—cucumber, rutabaga: song/ vegetable improv. /song /improv. etc. All vegetables improvise together at end.

## 14. BLUEBELLS COCKLESHELLS: Pitch matching, vegetable rhythms and shopping habits

Every music teacher needs a sturdy repertoire of pitch-matching games. Think of them as shooting practice in basketball. Sometimes we aim the ball too high or too low, sometimes we shoot just right and make the basket. The coach makes helpful suggestions about posture, ball grip, focus. Then we practice and we improve.

Singing is a skill like basketball, with one difference—sometimes young children can't tell whether they've made the basket or not. Our first step as teachers is to listen to the children sing one by one, but without making them feel self-conscious. Games like *Bluebells* give us a playful way to hear the children sing unaware that someone's listening. When they "miss the basket" the first time, I just note the problem without saying anything. In future classes, I coach the children to use their head voice (prepared in other exercises) or match them at their pitch and keep asking questions, raising the tone one step at a time. I also share the basketball image with them, countering the prevailing notion that you either can sing or you can't. All the children in my program eventually match pitch.

Always looking for ways to take the original game further, we look for speech/rhythm connections with an emphasis on vegetables, an idea that came after a sobering first grade class in which the children could choose anything to buy at the store. One after another chose Pokemon cards, Nike shoes, Barbie, Nintendo, Starbucks mocha frappucino with soy milk. Longing for the days when "Johnny wants a pair of skates, Susie wants a sled," I told them that this store doesn't carry brand-name products. When I called on the first student, he sat silently, chin in hand with furrowed brow for a full minute. The room was filled with drums, bells, scarves, chairs, but still he sat in silence, the mediated advertising more present in his mind than the objects around him. Finally, his neighbor whispered to him, "Drum" and his eyes lit up. So while I still sometimes check in to see what they *do* buy at the store, mostly I steer them to things without brand names—carrots, cucumbers, kale.

We then steer the vegetables toward melodic improvisation and before we know it, we have a full-blown activity complete with singing, drones and improvisation. What a productive trip to the store *that* turns out to be!

## Preparation

+ All sit in a circle with four instruments arranged in a square in the center—alto xylophone, soprano xylophone, alto metallophone, soprano glockenspiel. Teacher plays bass xylophone. Vegetables—real, fake, or pictures—are spread around room.
+ Tell a little story:

> "Once there was a little girl who was so happy that she sang all day long. When her parents needed her to go to the store, she was happy to do it. Her parents were so grateful for her helpful attitude they told her she could buy something for herself as well. On her way to the store, this is what she sang."

(All sing the song while one child walks around room and picks one of the vegetables, returns at the end and sits down at one of the instruments. Teacher accompanies with drone.)

+ Teacher (or later, the whole group) calls child's name and sings: "Nora, what did you buy at the store?" Nora sings (not speaks) what she bought—"Peppers." (If you want to hear more, you can ask leading questions, "Were they red peppers or green peppers?" "They were yellow peppers." "Thank you.")
+ All chant "Peppers, peppers, peppers, yum!" (2x)

Repeat as above, continue until four children are seated at the instruments.

+ All sing the song again and now the children at the instruments improvise (one at a time) a melody following the rhythm of their vegetable (see examples in score). Choose two more rhythmically complementary vegetables: cucumber, rutabaga. After each child has played alone, sing once more with all children playing together.

Repeat entire sequence with four more children. Remember to write something later about the quality of their singing and their compositional ideas on the xylophones.

### Variations

+ Have the children walk around the room and shop for percussion instruments. They play the name of their chosen instrument on the instrument:

  "Cowbell, cowbell, I bought a cowbell."

+ Instead of walking around the room to buy something, four children seated at the instruments freely improvise for 16 beats, showing how they "walked to the store" through their melody. This is an excellent way to assess each child's ability to create simple melodies. Is there a sense of pattern and repetition? Does he play with both hands? Can she sing what she played?

+ Use two or three vegetable names to improvise on three notes, C–D–E; two others using G–A–C. Combine them to play a longer melody (see example below).

# Vegetable Improvisation

Broc-co li broc-co-li  cu-cum-ber kale.  Broc-co-li broc-co-li  cu-cum-ber kale.

Cu-cum-ber kale.  Cu-cum-ber kale.  Broc-co-li broc-co-li  cu-cum-ber kale.

+ Extend the vegetable poem with adjectives. For example, a "pepper." What color is it? Is it crisp? Is it yummy? Now they can fashion little rhymes that focus the improvisation:

  "Red pepper, red pepper, crisp and yummy
  It tastes so good as it goes to my tummy."

# As I Was Going to St. Ives

As I was go-ing to St. Ives, I met a man with se-ven wives.

E-'vry wife had se-ven sacks. E-'vry sack had

se-ven cats. E-'vry cat had sev en kits.

Kits, cats, sacks, wives, how ma-ny go-ing to St. Ives? ONE!

## 15. ST. IVES: 7's and 8's, instrumental range, conscious composition and a riddle

The "hook" that drew me to this poem was the combination of the recurring seven's and intriguing image of the geometrically expanding (while diminishing in size) wives, sacks, cats, and kits. I was very proud of myself when I showed this to the first graders and began to draw the expanding pyramid on the board.

We got so involved that we went ten minutes over our time. When the first grade teacher came in demanding her children, I proudly showed her our work and suggested she could use class time to figure out the answer. She looked at me with a wry smile and said, "I already know." We sat with hushed anticipation and after a pregnant silence, she announced, "One. Because as I was going to St. Ives, the man I met was coming from the other direction!" * Which only goes to show that first grade teachers are much smarter than music teachers.

Meanwhile, the seven's are really eight's because seven notes are spread over eight pulses. This suggests some rhythmic improvisational work with eight. With eight notes in an octave, it also suggests a melodic connection (which we will modify with our pentatonic scale). Finally, with the range of size from wives to kits, this text is begging us to enlighten the children about the families of instruments, from bass to soprano.

### The Performance
+ Make a circle of percussion instruments in the center, four of each kind ranging from low to high (four hand drums, four woodblocks, four cowbells, four shakers).
+ Sing the rhyme and all clap seven times after each phrase. Repeat, differentiating the pitch of the claps, from low to high.
+ Invite rhythmic variation within the above structures.
+ Have children speculate on the relation between size of instruments in the center and pitch. Demonstrate and discuss, labeling them bass, tenor, alto, soprano.
+ Pass out four drums to the first four children in the circle. Each plays rhythmic variation as above at appropriate place in the poem. Pass out the next group of four instruments. Continue until all have an instrument.
+ Standing, those with the largest instruments take seven steps into center while playing rhythmic variation (after "seven wives") followed by next highest sound and so on. All jump back playing one sound on appropriate word ("Kits, cats, sacks, wives").

### Orff Instruments
+ Apply "big to small" to Orff instruments. (Note that there is no "tenor" instrument and that the soprano glockenspiel is an octave higher than the soprano xylophone.)
+ In C pentatonic, play from low C to high C counting the notes (6). Double one note to make it fit the "seven" format (see arrangement).
+ Create a drama with some on percussion walking to St. Ives while others play Orff instruments. All "dancers" jump and turn at the end while exclaiming "One!"

---

* Some say "none," because technically the riddle asks how many kits, cats, sacks, wives are going. Others suggest that you could meet the man and his entourage at a crossroads and they also are going to St. Ives. In which case you have the narrator, the man, seven wives, 49 sacks, 343 cats, 2,401 kittens, for a grand total of 2,802. And parenthetically, the Cornwall, England Tourist Board highly recommends that you go to St. Ives, a beautiful seaside town.

# Charlie Wag

V1: What kind of pud-ding did he eat?

V2: What kind of pud-ding did he eat?

V3: One was bread,

V4: and the oth-er meat.

AX: Char-lie Wag, Char-lie Wag, Ate the pud-ding and

AG: Wag, Char-lie Wag, Char-lie Wag, he

BX:

V1: Plum pud-ding     Plum pud-ding

V2: Rice pud-ding     Rice pud-ding

V3: Bread pud-ding

V4: Meat pud-ding.

## 16. CHARLIE WAG: Complementary rhythm and motion, one-bar composition and a potpourri of puddings

Adult songs lean toward love, but nursery rhymes are enamored with food. Charlie Wag joins Betty Botter, Davy Davy Dumpling, Hannah Bantry, Jack Sprat, Little Miss Muffet, Peter Piper and a host of other hungry characters in this homage to pudding. (Perhaps at the end of this nursery rhyme study, a feast of pudding, plums, peppers, curds and whey would be in order!)

We associate puddings with dessert, but they can be savory or sweet and the original word, from the French "boudin," refers to sausage (the bag in the rhyme may refer to the sausage casing or the English practice of making the pudding in a bag). Puddings can be baked, boiled or steamed and run the gamut from meat puddings (the Scottish haggis, English steak and kidney pudding, Spanish morcilla) to grain puddings (Yiddish noodle kugel, Chinese rice pudding, Puerto Rican bread pudding) to fruit puddings (English plum pudding and figgy pudding) to vegetable puddings (Appalachian corn pudding, English peas pudding found in a variant nursery rhyme "Peas pudding hot") to the many sweet versions—flan, mousse, custard, chocolate and beyond.

A fun way to begin this class is to put a plum, a piece of bread, a small bag of rice and a sausage inside each of four bags and have the children feel inside and guess what kind of pudding it is. This prepares the accompanying ostinato chant.

### Teaching the Piece
- Teach the first, second and fourth measures of the melody, speaking the third measure.
- Transfer to xylophones; click mallets on spoken phrase.
- Starting on G, each decides how to play spoken phrase. Listen to various solutions (two are given in the score) and choose two or three for everyone to play.
- Note how the text of the second line rhythmically complements the melodic rhythm. Note how the counter-melody moves in the opposite direction of the main melody.
- Double select percussion instruments with speaking parts.
- Perform entire arrangement.

# Doctor Foster

## Sample solo

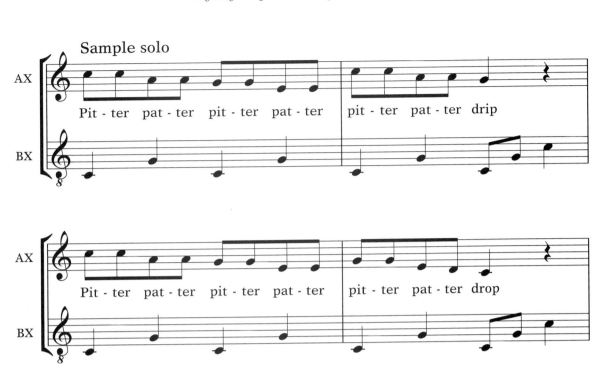

AX — Pit - ter pat - ter pit - ter pat - ter | pit - ter pat - ter drip

BX

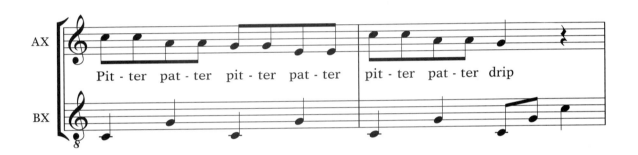

AX — Pit - ter pat - ter pit - ter pat - ter | pit - ter pat - ter drop

BX

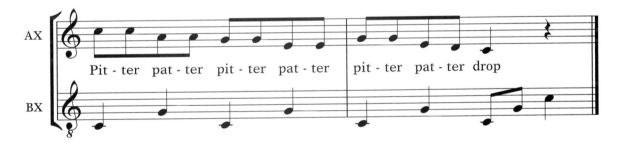

AX — Pit - ter pat - ter pit - ter pat - ter | pit - ter pat - ter drip

BX

AX — Pit - ter pat - ter pit - ter pat - ter | pit - ter pat - ter drop

BX

Children "pitter-patter" on Dr. Foster's umbrella.

## 17. DOCTOR FOSTER: Seven again, color parts, descending and ascending phrases and good health care

Most children—and young teachers—will be astounded to hear that doctors once made house calls—even in the rain! Such tidbits of information are found throughout nursery rhymes, teaching us a bit of history as well as vital linguistic and musical skills.

This arrangement is clear and simple, a full-blown five-note pentatonic melody begging for color parts and supported by two kinds of drones. The seven-note pattern found in *St. Ives* is now descending (into the puddle) from the highest note instead of ascending. By starting on the high A, we come to rest comfortably on the G at the end, preparing for the final cadence (a foreshadowing of the V-I endings students will play in five or six years).

### Extensions

Select students make a "puddle" by forming a circle touching mallets with neighbors. They circle around singing the song while one student (Doctor Foster) walks outside of them carrying an umbrella. Students in the circle stop and raise mallets on "he stepped in a puddle" while Doctor Foster steps into the circle and sinks down into the puddle. Doctor Foster stays crouched under the umbrella while students in circle tap gently on top of the umbrella, reciting and following the rhythm of "Pitter patter pitter patter pitter patter drip, pitter patter pitter patter pitter patter drop." Meanwhile, one student improvises a melody to the above text at the same time. Continue with a new Doctor Foster.

Doctor Foster sinking into the puddle.

# Bow Wow Wow

Bow wow wow    Whose dog art thou?

Lit-tle Tom-my Tuck-er's dog    Bow wow wow    Bow wow wow.

**18. BOW WOW WOW: The return of Tommy Tucker's dog, with an optional body percussion part**

Remember Tommy's dog? He's back with a new bark—the sweet sounds of the Orff instruments, coupled with the deep "woof" of the color part on the contra-bass bars and another version of Keith Terry's versatile ideas. It's all classic elemental forms, with the kind of driving ostinato that Orff and Keetman favored (but not so by many American Orff arrangers) and a clear melody that uses the full range of the pentatonic scale.

Consider using this instrumental version as the A section of a rondo with the body percussion parts explored earlier as B, C and D sections. This arrangement also makes a great companion piece to *One Two Three* introduced later.

First grader playing the pentatonic scale.

# Old Man Mosie

### 19. OLD MAN MOSIE: Moving drones, swing rhythm and homegrown therapy

In this delightful rhyme, Mother Goose crosses the tracks and meets her cousin, Old Man Mosie, who shows her how to loosen up and wiggle her hips. Most of the rhymes in this book are from our Anglo heritage but similar rhymes can be found throughout the world and within our own diverse culture as well. Similar, but also distinctly different and how delicious those differences are! Many of them are in my book *Now's the Time: Teaching Jazz to All Ages,* so here I include just a few from our African-American heritage.

This rhyme has yet another doctor offering sage advice: when you're feeling down, a bit "sick in the head," step forward, turn around (as the Shaker's sang, "to turn and to turn will be our delight, 'till by turning, turning, we come 'round right.") and get out of town.

That's deep. Instead of talking to the therapist about your mother, you could look at your feelings in a larger social context. Perhaps you drive alone on a crowded freeway and then work all day in a little cubicle with stale air and poor lighting. You go home to a pre-prepared genetically-modified dinner and then sit by yourself in front of the TV at night watching Judge Judy. No wonder you're depressed! The doctor says, "Don't sit there and whine. *Get up and do something!* Volunteer for moveon.org. Plant a garden. Tutor a child. Travel. Dance the Hokey Pokey—what if it really *is* what it's all about?"

Meanwhile, back in class, the kids are discovering how Orff orchestration embraces many styles. The drone now moves, alternating G and A, the melody is a singable and playable pentatonic tune, the color part and ostinato swing like jazz riffs. Just changing from straight to swing rhythm, shifting from beat to offbeat, and syncopating the melody, will have a powerful musical effect. And while we needn't call Mother Goose square or Old Man Mosie hip (each has its own beauty and character), you may find American children responding in quite a different way to these sounds that reveal a profound part of their cultural identity.

### Extensions

It's not enough to just play these pieces on the instruments. With the Orff approach, we prepare them on the body, activate them with dance, games, movement, drama, and then put all the parts together in a multi-faceted performance, and thus achieve a much higher level of engagement.

I like to begin with a rhythmic warm-up using body percussion to get us swingin'. The two patterns below work well. Everyone learns both and then form two groups to play them together:

+ After practicing the above patterns, choose a partner and play both patterns together.
+ Sing the song as a clapping play with a partner.
+ Performer on part 2 is Old Man Mosie, part 1, the Doctor. Sing the song and make appropriate motions.
+ Old Man Mosie leaves partner and continues body percussion, moving on the steps in search of a new doctor who continues in place. After four cycles, all have a new partner. Repeat as often as desired. For variation, on the moving section all sing, "I need a doctor, I need a doctor now," to the ostinato in the bass xylophone.

- All move to instruments and find the melody and ostinato they were singing.
- Add the hi-hat and ride cymbal, as shown below:

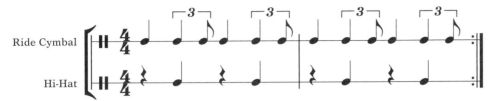

- Review all above, with half of the class playing instruments, others performing with partner as above. Switch.

**SUGGESTED FORM:**

A    Sing the song accompanied only by bass and hi-hat. Both continue throughout.

B    Body percussion while finding new doctor. Add bass ostinato and ride cymbal.

A$^1$    Play melody on xylophones. Add color part.

B    As in B above, but some singing "I need a doctor…"

A$^2$    Play all parts while singing.

This challenging arrangement is best for 2$^{nd}$ graders at the end of the year or third graders at the beginning. It's a wonderful example of both the universality and the versatility of the basic principles of drone, ostinato, color and pentatonic melody.

"Old Man Mosie" examining the doctor's pill.

# The Donkey

feed him some corn. The best lit-tle don-key that ev- er was born!

## 20. THE DONKEY: Hee-haws, multi-mallet technique and kindness to animals

I tried to suggest the donkey's gritty "Hee-Haw" in this arrangement, but on these euphonious instruments, it's no easy task (listen to the violins hee-haw in Saint- Saens' *Carnival of the Animals* for contrast). In the pentatonic scale, the interval of the second gives the greatest dissonance and I use it here not only in the introduction, but also in the modified drone. Both require two mallets in one hand, an intriguing challenge for those just learning mallet technique.

The melody lies in the top half of the pentatonic scale and offers a challenge to sing the high E. Some vocal warm-ups with ascending patterns will both help prepare the children and tell you whose range comfortably fits the melody. If you save this piece for an age when kids have started recorder (3rd grade in our school), it's a friendly melody for the soprano recorder, again with a high E challenge.

As for the text, the rhyme defies the "spare the rod, spoil the child" notion—better to provide shelter, food and the faith that this donkey, this child, surely must be "the best one that ever was born." *

---

* In Nicholas Nickleby, a doctor tells a father that his newborn baby is "The finest boy I ever saw in my whole life." Dickens comments, "It is a pleasant thing to reflect upon, and furnishes a complete answer to those who contend for the gradual degeneration of the human species, that every baby born into the world is a finer one than the last."

A farmer and his donkey.

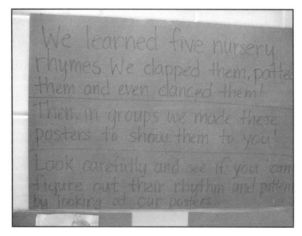

A notation project by Talia Goodkin.

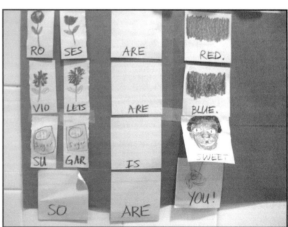

Notation project continued.

# Introducing Pentatonic Modes: Re and La

The next three pieces feature two modal versions of the pentatonic scale and need some special preparation. At my school, we introduce this new concept in second grade. It is an exciting moment, for teachers and students alike, when we triple our expressive power simply by shifting our tonal center up, or down, one note.

One child-friendly way to introduce the pentatonic modes is through a little story:

> Carl, Debby and Alex were playing happily one day at Carl's house. (Children play a C pentatonic song or improvisation.) Suddenly they heard a scream. Carl's Dad had discovered a termite! He instantly called the exterminators and told the children they would have to play somewhere else. So they all went next door to Debby's house.

(All the parts shift up one note—basses now playing a D and A drone, ostinato relating to these two tones and melody and improvisations ending on D).

> Because they lived in an old neighborhood where no two houses were alike, things felt different at Debby's house. They played happily for a while and then decided to see if it was okay to go back to Carl's. (Switch back to C and play for short time). But it was still kind of smelly from the spraying, so they went back to Debby's. Soon the fumes started to come over to Debby's house, so they decided to go to Alex's house. They had to pass the neighbor's house and an empty lot to get there. (All shift to A as the home tone). After a while they went back to Carl's and played until they had to go home for dinner.

When they shift from one tonal center to another in this manner, the children can hear dramatic differences in these three modes. Now they need to understand *why* the sound changes. One possibility is to write the notes on the board to see the difference.

## Pentatonic Modes—Do, Re, La

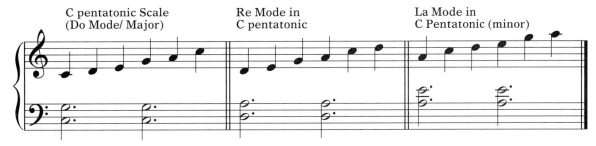

At an adult level, we can show and describe how the interval structure of the scale changes, but a more kid-friendly version is another little story with a graphic image—the water bottles on a hot day.

Line up five kids to form a "living pentatonic scale," with a gap between the 3rd and 4th child. Give the 1st a big water bottle, the 4th a medium one and the 3rd a small one. Each child represents one tone in the scale, starting with Do. Seated children sing the scale while teacher puts hand over each head of the "living scale." Then comes the explanation.

> Imagine it's a very hot day and five friends are together. One has a big water bottle, one a medium one, one has a small one and two don't have anything. Who is the most important person in this arrangement?

The Do pentatonic scale with water bottles.

Another day, different people have the water bottles. It's the same five people standing in the same order, but now the two that were very unimportant before are suddenly very important—it's the *relationships* that have changed.

The Re mode.

On still another day, the relationships shift again. That's how the modes work—the same five notes, but a different "home tone" each time, supported by a different drone.

La mode.

This study of pentatonic modes will help prepare the later study of diatonic modes, which follow essentially the same principle.

# Old King Cole

called    for    his    fid - d' - lers     three.

The fiddlers three.

## 21. OLD KING COLE: Re mode, multiple drones and fiddles

This setting was inspired by some violin students I had in second grade years ago. We used it in a drama and you haven't seen cute until you've seen three seven-year-old boys dressed in court finery sawing away on their little fiddles.

The Re mode is found in folk literature; singer Jean Ritchie has a version of this song in this mode but with a different melody. The accompaniment is almost entirely drones of different tempos and textures, with a few C's thrown in for color.

With so many folk and fairy tales inhabited by Kings and Queens, consider folding this, along with the upcoming *Queen Caroline*, into a drama. It's a good moment to search out the violin players in your school and invite them to join the Orff ensemble—the sound of the violin fits well with the Orff instruments. It is fun for the violin students to show off their skills and also refreshing for them to play away from the page, find melodies by ear and even improvise a bit.

### Form

- Sing the song twice through with accompaniment.
- Add a spoken section, vigorously chanted, with percussion punctuation on underlined words: "*Bring* me my pipe! *Bring* me my bowl! *Bring* me my fiddlers three!"
- Fiddlers enter playing the famous Suzuki ostinato, "Mississippi hot dog" (Where did *that* come from?). They can divide the D and A amongst them or play both open strings.

One of the fiddlers, along with some solo alto and soprano xylophones, plays the melody with above ostinati added to the Orff instrument accompaniment.
- All continue to play while singing the song once more.

# One Two Three

One two three. Moth-er caught a flea.

Flea died, moth-er cried. One two three. three.

## 22. ONE, TWO, THREE: La mode, melodic notation and composition, funeral music and the Buddhist principle of "ahimsa"

People often associate the La mode, which can properly be called a minor pentatonic scale, with sadness. It's true that the minor third can evoke a moody, sometimes haunting quality, but one of the saddest songs I know, *Go Tell Aunt Rhody*, is entirely in the major scale while some of the most joyful songs and games, like the African-American ring play *Soup Soup*, are often sung in minor pentatonic. There are simply too many factors—rhythm, tempo, text, timbre, etc.—to say that the minor mode is sad.

But with the right text and tempo, the minor mode can help create an inward and yes, sad, feeling. This rhyme is whimsical to us, but the Jains of India hold that all living things, down to the smallest creatures, have a soul and thus, are worthy of respect and protection. That may seem extreme (especially when camping with mosquitoes), but it is certainly a point of view worth sharing with children.

Japan's premier haiku poet, Issa (1763–1828) took to heart the Buddhist principle of "ahimsa" (avoiding harm to all creatures as much as possible) when he wrote these haiku:

| | | |
|---|---|---|
| O flea! | For you fleas too | Do not kill the fly! |
| Don't jump whatever you do | The night must be long. | See how it wrings its hands |
| That way is the River Sumida | It must be lonely. | Its feet! |

That said, I still do this with tongue in cheek, telling how mother picked the fleas off Tommy Tucker's dog hoping to enroll them in a flea re-location program. But in her zeal she squeezed too hard and one flea died. So we got hired to play the funeral music and off we go in our minor pentatonic song. After playing the melody twice, the soloist delivers the eulogy while the accompaniment continues.

> "We are gathered here to mourn the passing of our friend, Mr. Flea. He was a good provider for his family, always sharing the blood he sucked with his little ones. He was also an excellent jumper and once leaped from a Chihuahua to a St. Bernard in a single bound. He will be sadly missed."

I recently used this rhyme as a springboard to melodic composition. Instead of teaching the melody as given in the arrangement, each child created his or her own melody on the Orff instruments following four simple suggestions:

1) Start and end on A.
2) Follow the rhythm of the text.
3) Practice it until you can remember it.
4) Make sure you can sing what you composed.

The children were spread around the room working on their ideas. When they felt finished, they played their composition for me and I notated it. They then had to copy my notation (see below). When all were finished, I took the notated pieces to the piano and played them one by one twice through. The children had to recognize their own melody and then play with me the second time.

This simple lesson is effective on multiple levels:

1) Children creating their own melodies are working at a high level of musical cognition, demonstrating what they understand about phrase and structure.
2) Carl Orff once said that teaching notation begins with children notating their own compositions. Here is that process in action, the children both motivated and fascinated by the process of creating symbolic representations of their work.
3) Children experience first-hand how notation can both preserve their musical memory and communicate to those not in the room. (I took their compositions to a teacher work-

shop and had adults play them, filmed it and showed the kids the grown-ups playing their compositions. Imagine the smiles on the kids' faces!)

4) Copying over my notation is a first-step in eventually learning to notate themselves, prepared by other classes in reading and writing rhythm and pitch.

5) Children note how no two melodies are the same (though several began the same way) and understand the range of creative possibility.

Here are some of their sample melodies:

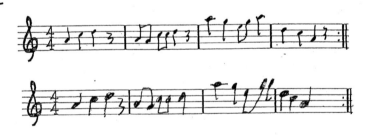

ONE TWO THREE      MO-THER CAUGHT A FLEA

FLEA DIED, MO-THER CRIED   ONE TWO THREE

Name Megan

ONE TWO THREE      MO-THER CAUGHT A FLEA

FLEA DIED, MO-THER CRIED   ONE TWO THREE

Name Anne

ONE TWO THREE      MO-THER CAUGHT A FLEA

FLEA DIED, MO-THER CRIED   ONE TWO THREE

Name Gordon

Name Jack

ONE TWO THREE    MO–THER CAUGHT A FLEA

FLEA DIED, MO–THER CRIED   ONE TWO THREE

Name Brisa

ONE TWO THREE    MO–THER CAUGHT A FLEA

FLEA DIED, MO–THER CRIED   ONE TWO THREE

Name Anja

ONE TWO THREE    MO–THER CAUGHT A FLEA

FLEA DIED, MO–THER CRIED   ONE TWO THREE

# Davy Davy Dumpling—Kitchen Version

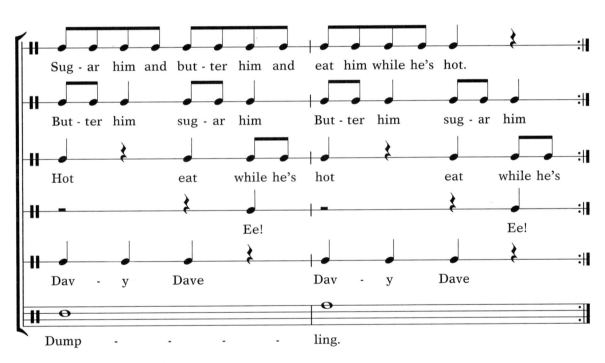

# Davy Davy Dumpling

2nd grade students—SF School

## RE mode

### 23. DAVY DAVY DUMPLING: Review of Do, La, Re modes, binary form, kitchen instruments and the musical genius of kids

Whereas the kids worked alone to create melodies in "One, Two, Three," here my second graders worked in groups of four to create all the parts to the music. I divided the class into three groups, one for each mode and said: "Choose four Orff instruments, decide who plays drone, ostinato, color or melody, begin to invent your part (in conversation with the others), clarify the form and practice. You have fifteen minutes and then we'll share."

If you've ever doubted the musical genius of kids, consider the results demonstrated in the examples shown. Given a clear structure and form, armed with relevant conceptual knowledge and sufficient technique, practiced in collaborating with others (all achieved through the Orff approach), the kids come through with flying colors. A few details worth noticing:

- The different flavors of our "modal dumplings" and variety of melodic shapes.
- The solo B section (either the kids arrived at this independently or were stealing the idea from each other—a kind of thievery I heartily endorse in music class!).
- The outlaw drone in the La mode piece (with 5th below tonic on the second half of each measure)—and it works just fine.
- Most intriguing is the 10- beat ostinato on the metallophone in the Do version that crosses the 4/4 meter. Not only did the melody player know exactly where to come in, but the ostinato player intuitively compensated at the end of the phrase.

In performance, we began with the speech version, both spoken and played with "kitchen instruments." (I strongly recommend a bundt pan for one of the bowls.) In between every section is a rondo filler: "Sugar him and butter him and eat him while he's hot." *

---

* My colleague, James Harding, insists it should be "butter him, sugar him" so the sugar will stick. Technically, he's correct, but all versions I've found have it reversed. To heed James' culinary wisdom, I re-ordered the ostinato part.

# Intermediate Arrangements—2nd to 4th Grade

**Transposition: C–F–G, 6/8 meter, soprano recorder**

In this section, we encounter intermediate pieces, new concepts and new instruments. Some are playable by second graders, but most are written with third graders in mind. With a few years of xylophone technique, elemental orchestration, and ensemble skills under their belts, they are ready to play more challenging pieces and also begin a new study—the soprano recorder. Many of the pieces integrate recorder, a common Orff practice.

Before moving on to the next big concept in their melodic/harmonic development— transposition—students can review C pentatonic in 6/8 meter, enjoy a large integrated performance, play more modal arrangements, swing another jazz arrangement and then challenge their technical skills on our up tempo exercise in transposition, *Peter Piper*.

In some ways, the concept of transposition is easier than the modal concept. You can bring up the five kids with the water bottles again (Do version) and then have them simply walk four steps forward. Their relationships with each other stay the same, but now they have a different spatial relationship to the room itself. Another way to show it would be to have the five sit in a chair (C pentatonic), then stand up (F pentatonic), then stand on the chair (G pentatonic).

The new concepts in third grade, amply represented in the pieces chosen, are as follows:

+ **Rhythm:** sixteenth notes; triplets; 6/8 meter
+ **Melody:** C, F and G pentatonic (transposed)
+ **Harmony:** Double moving drone

# Hickory Dickory Dock

Hick-o-ry dick-o-ry dock__ The mouse ran up the clock__ The

clock struck one, The mouse ran down. Hick-o-ry dick-o-ry dock.__

## 24. HICKORY DICKORY DOCK: 6/8 meter, choreography and music without melody

All the rhymes up to this point have been set in 2/4 or 4/4 (*Moses Supposes* excepted). The natural habitat of most nursery rhymes is 6/8, but I have purposefully changed them to make them more accessible for xylophones (the three strokes per beat in 6/8 are challenging when using 2 mallets). 2/4 and 4/4 are also more friendly for learning rhythmic notation in first and second grade. (For more on teaching notation see French Time-Name system in my book *Play, Sing and Dance*.) The third graders are ready to play and notate 6/8 pieces.

*Hickory Dickory Dock* (along with *The Cow, Two Tutors, The House That Jack Built, Humpty Dumpty, The Lion and the Unicorn, Sally Go 'Round the Sun*) is one of the rhymes that has not been metrically altered. It features Keith Terry's patterns, now transposed to 6/8, introduces the characteristic color part of the meter (boom, boom!), harks back to the old "say, play, say-play" formula, and brings canon back into the mix.

This arrangement, from 1984, eventually made its way around the Orff circuit. Once, after doing a different body percussion piece in a workshop, someone came up to me bubbling with enthusiasm, said, "This is just like this cool piece someone taught me!" and then showed me my own *Hickory Dickory Dock*. "That's very interesting," I said thinking, "It's time to publish this material." Here it is, 24 years later!

### Teaching Suggestions

+ March to various 6/8 tunes looking for places where you can clap twice.

  "The noble Duke of York (clap clap) He had ten thousand men (clap clap)…"
  "The ants go marching one by one, hurrah (clap clap), hurrah (clap clap)…"
  "Sally go round the chimney pots, every afternoon (clap clap)…"

+ Students find other rhymes that invite two claps. If *Hickory Dickory Dock* is chosen, proceed as below. If not, suggest it.
+ Recite text with double claps. Speak in two-part canon.
+ Practice the body percussion part as shown in score. Speak text, play text, speak and play. Repeat in two-part canon.
+ Practice the above with two groups standing and facing each other about ten feet apart. Playing a tick-tock on a double woodblock, all mime a wooden figure marching in place (cuckoo clock). All recite the poem and move toward middle, then play body percussion, then play and speak, moving backward on the two steps. Repeat in canon.
+ Teach instrumental parts. Take time to clarify the concept of "moving drone." In *Old Man Mosie*, the upper note swings back and forth between G and A—in this piece, it's the lower note moving from C to D. Note the "tick-tock" of the woodblock and the way the glockenspiel changes direction when the mouse runs down. (This can also be played as an ascending, then descending, glissando, with the characteristic color rhythm played by a cowbell).
+ Instruments enter every two measures in the following order: woodblock, BX, AX, SX, AX, S/AG. Dancers move in place. When all instruments are in, perform as shown above. After the canon, instruments drop out in reverse order.

# The Cow

Jack Prelutsky
arranged by Doug Goodkin

The cow mainly moos as she chooses to moo.
And she chooses to moo as she chooses.
She furthermore chews as she chooses to chew,
And she chooses to chew as she muses.
If she chooses to chew she may moo as she chews.
Or may chew just to chew as she muses.
If she chooses to moo she may moo to amuse,
Or may moo just to moo as she chooses.

### 25. THE COW: Homonyms, assonance, sequence and toy cows

Here is a different kind of 6/8 feel, a cowboy-amble appropriate to the subject matter. Like a cow look-ing for new grass, we've strayed from the Mother Goose herd and into the field of children's poetry, this one by the always-imaginative Jack Prelutsky. The marvelous play between the homonyms "choose" and "chews," "muse," "moos" and "amuse," gets the children ruminating on the assonant vowel sounds like a cow chewing its cud. The toy cow (those little cylinders that moo when you turn them over) adds extra zest to an already humorous poem. Note that the percussion parts in the score are divided amongst four children. Like *Hickory Dickory Dock*, there is no melody to this poem, just the underlying ostinati that accompany the text.

While perfectly delicious to teach just as it is, this poem is also great for getting the kids involved in word-smithing. Copy these lines and cut them into eight separate strips.

+ She chooses to moo as she chooses
+ Or may chew just to chew as she muses
+ The cow mainly moos as she chooses to moo
+ She chooses to chew as she muses
+ If she chooses to moo she may moo to amuse
+ She furthermore chews as she chooses to chew
+ Or may moo just to moo as she chooses
+ If she chooses to chew she may moo as she chews

+ Pass out a complete set to small groups and have them put the lines in order.
+ Each group shares their solution. Show the original poem, compare solutions and recite.

### FORM:
+ Unaccompanied recitation, one line per child
+ Bass—four measures; unpitched percussion—8 measures; repeat poem
+ Bass continues three more measures and ends on C. End with free toy cow sounds.

# Come Butter Come

**26. COME BUTTER COME: More moving drones, creamy texture, integrated performance and the pleasure of patience**

You can't make butter cake without butter and this rhyme hearkens back to the days when butter was freshly churned at home. Peter is hungry for dessert and waiting impatiently for it. In this setting of the rhyme, the other children gather around as well, the simple melody surrounded by a dense and challenging accompaniment. To give the effect of butter thickening, one new ostinato can be added for each repeat of the A section. However, feel free to decline the banquet and just nibble—delete or change some of the ostinati to suit your needs or just play the song and skip the dramatic development. Remember that all of these settings and suggestions are simply possibilities to be adapted and adopted by you and your students.

I enjoyed imagining the children waiting impatiently for the butter and rondo form was the perfect way to extend the piece and make them wait. Here is your chance to revisit some of the pieces we did in Part One. For large classes, divide the group so that each part contributes to the whole. If you teach two or three sections of one grade level, you could forego the "Teach all the parts to everyone" rule and give separate sections to each group. The basic structure is as follows:

- **A section:** One child "churns the butter," playing the beat in either a real butter churn (hard to come by) or a simulated one (baseball bat and bucket?) while a small group gathers round and sings the song. Another group plays the instrumental accompaniments, beginning with just drone and melody.
- **B section:** During the "la la" singing, the children skip away and gather "offstage."
- **C section:** Orff instruments stop and the group above performs a clapping game to pass the time while waiting (as in *Choco-la-te* from Part One.) Churner keeps playing beat.
- **A section:** Instruments begin again with a new group of children around the butter churner. Add another ostinato part to thicken the texture.
- **B section:** As above, to a different "offstage" location.
- **D section:** As above, with new game (as in *Ice Cream Soda* jump rope).
- **Repeat entire sequence for as needed for additional groups.** (Next group can play *Engine Engine* as a counting out game, another bounce balls to *Days of the Week*, etc.
- **Final A:** All groups circle around the butter churner again and entire ensemble slows down as the butter gets harder to churn. At the end, all lean in, put their fingers in the butter churn, and lick them on the final octave C.

This is the first offering here of a kind of drama that brings all the threads together. A production such as this might take months to prepare, learning the techniques of body percussion, singing, mallet work, a variety of games and social skills in group settings.

I call these little dramas "integrated performances" and they are a refreshing way to have your cake and eat it too—not a dull recital or exhibition of exercises, but fresh buttercake! Here process and performance are not separate, but connected, the latter growing organically out of the former. The children, natives in the land of story, feel right at home and are always thrilled to use their musical talents to tell this little tale. This kind of production echoes some of Orff's stage works, which integrate music, dance and drama in his own eclectic style. (His masterpiece, *Carmina Burana*, is often called a "scenic cantata.")

# Jack Sprat

V/R

licked          the          plat - ter          clean.

Glock.

SX

SM

AX

BX

BM

## 27. JACK SPRAT: Stretching the drone, Re mode, complementary rhythms and compatible relationships

For me, every piece in this book is a doorway into remembering the children who played it and the feeling we had—so much more than a combination of pleasing notes. *Jack Sprat* is the first piece I arranged in Re-mode and was featured on the first recording I made of the kids in my school back in 1983 (see accompanying CD).

Each ostinato part is taught by text derived from the rhyme, but placed in such a way as to avoid parallel rhythms. A summary:

| | | | | |
|---|---|---|---|---|
| G: | | no lean | | no fat |
| SX: | Couldn't eat fat | | Couldn't eat lean | |
| SM: | Jack | Sprat | Jack | Sprat |
| AX: | Wife could eat no lean | | His wife could eat no lean | His… |
| BM: | Jack | Sprat | Jack | Sprat |
| BX: | Eat no fat | Eat no lean | Eat no fat | Eat no lean |

A close look at the score reveals some departures from our strict rules of drones. The A and E drone on beat four violates the rule restricting first and fifth degree to the strong beats and seems to imply an inverted V chord. Yet, in the listening it's clear that the bass part functions more like a moving drone than a I-V progression. As a fledgling Orff orchestrator, I seemed to be following Duke Ellington's dictum, "If it sounds good, it is good." We thought it sounded good.

The range of the melody is a stretch for the beginning recorder student, but might be a good solo opportunity for a precocious student. To extend the song, I would suggest melodic improvisations.

The dramatic route is another possibility for introducing or extending the piece. The musical focus of complementary rhythms reflects the text—Jack and his wife (alas, she has no name!) have a perfectly balanced relationship that leaves their plates clean at the end of the meal.

Follow the theme by searching for opposites that don't compete but complement. Have kids create skits or movement studies showing this at work, with the above piece as the A section of a rondo. Some examples:

- A person with a high voice and low voice argue about where to begin a melody. The one with the low voice creates a complementary part below the melody and it sounds better than before. Or they sing it an octave apart.
- A tall person wants to be shorter and a short person wants to be taller so they team up on a treasure hunt, one looking on the high shelves, the other under the furniture.
- The classroom teacher and music teacher work together: their complementary skills help the kids avoid an all-fat or all-lean diet.

# Grandpa Grigg

Gran'-pa Grigg, Had a pig, In a field of clov - er.

Glockenspiel

Alto
Xylophone

Bass
Xylophone

Bass
Metallophone

Pig - gy died, Gran'-pa cried, All the fun is ov - er.

Glock.

BX

BM

Gran'-pa Grigg, Had a pig, In a field of clov - er.

Pig - gy died, Gran'-pa cried, All the fun is ov - er.

## 28. GRANDPA GRIGG: Double moving drone, Re mode, counter-melody and affection for pigs

This charming arrangement illustrates an exciting new concept—the *double moving drone*. We've used the single-moving drone from the 5th to the 6th in *Old Man Mosie* and *The Cow*, from the 1st to the 2nd in *Hickory Dickory Dock* and soon, *Peter Piper*, but it's also possible to move both the upper and lower notes of the drone up to make a double moving drone. In the Re mode, they can move down in reverse, as follows:

While the above examples are bona fide drones (they set an unchanging foundation and add color), *Grandpa Grigg*, by shifting to C and G in the bass when the melody shifts to E and C, takes a first step toward functional harmony. Technically, this is a I VII chord change characteristic of much modal music (particularly in the Dorian, Mixolydian and Aeolian modes) and an older variant of the I-V cadence. But this is too much information for both the children and the Orff teacher who hasn't taken Level II, so just play it as written and know that you're preparing the ear for later understanding.

Meanwhile, the B section features a second melody following the rhythm of the text accompanied neither by drone or ostinato, but by a counter-melody that features complementary rhythm and contrary motion, thus expanding the resources of our young composers.

Finally, Grandpa, like the mother in *One, Two, Three*, is yet another sensitive soul who properly mourns the passing of his pig. The setting is neither funereal nor excessively happy, but it is certainly energetic. Enjoy!

# Queen Caroline

Tur-pen-tine    made   it   shine.    Queen    Queen    Car-o-line.

## 29. QUEEN CAROLINE—Moving drone in La mode, recorder, elemental Bolero and dubious hair products

Here we are back in La mode, with a texture that thickens over time (like each application of turpentine?). The three-note melody is well-suited for the beginning recorder student and indeed, the whole piece is based on those notes, the drones following their pattern with dubious parallel octaves, but strong reinforcement of the basic melodic shape.

The arrangement is modeled on Ravel's *Bolero,* thickening the texture by adding one or two parts for each reprise of the melody. Teach all the parts to the children (always singing the melody over the given drone or ostinato), divide up according to instruments and create an order of entrance. Once a part is in, it stays in. Begin with the alto xylophone part and bring the snare drum in last, moving from longer to shorter note values. When a new part enters, let it play two to four measures before the melody enters again. Each time the melody enters, add another melodic instrument as well (a good time to integrate the violin or clarinet or even piano). As the intensity builds through the increase in instruments and texture, you may add a crescendo for yet more power. Then play a recording of *Bolero* and watch the kids' amazement, "Hey! He stole our idea!"

This rhyme may refer to a real Caroline, wife of George, Prince of Wales. According to one source, she was "unhealthy and unhygienic." Since washing hair with turpentine was a folk remedy for getting rid of lice, this might explain the ridicule in the rhyme. After various scandals on both sides of the marriage, she left to live on the Continent, returning in 1820 when George was crowned King. He was not anxious to see her, but apparently the public turned out in support. One image for this arrangement could be the Queen walking through the streets with more and more people gathering in her favor, protesting that if she did use turpentine, it was simply to make her hair shiny.

# One, Two, Three—Jazz Version

## 30. ONE, TWO, THREE (Jazz Version): Riffs, syncopation, swing and a flea funeral, New Orleans style

After "mother caught a flea," we "got out of town" with Old Man Mosie and went all the way to New Orleans for a different kind of funeral. You know how that goes—a slow dirge on the way to the graveyard (the La version of our earlier arrangement) and an exuberant jazz tune on the way back (this setting). The Orff instruments aren't exactly the brass band, but the two faces of elemental composition—one inspired by West Europe, the other by West Africa—should both be present in the classroom. I suggest combining the two arrangements in a little drama.

Musically-speaking, the drone is gone altogether, although the bass riffs still keep it tied down to one tonality, the ostinati and melody are syncopated and the drums give the arrangement a jazz-rock feel.

2nd grade jazz singers and dancers.

# The North Wind

## 31. THE NORTH WIND—Mi mode, 3/4 meter, octave drone, recorder and compassion for robins

Practically speaking, the Mi mode doesn't exist. Or more precisely, it is theoretical rather than functional. I've researched folk songs of many cultures and the closest example I've found is a Javanese gamelan piece called *Ricik-Ricik*. The absence of the 5th degree creates two problems—first, it's impossible to accompany with an open 5th drone and secondly, hard to find melodies without the 5th as a point of rest (there are many three and four note melodies, in Bulgaria, for example, without 5ths, but then the 5th is either sounded or implied in the drone). There are some melodies that start or end on Mi, but they tend to be what are called plagal melodies in the La mode.

Undaunted by the lack of folkloric Mi mode melodies, I set off to create my own many years back and this is the result. The modified drone uses the octave, reinforced in the color part. The four-note melody is easily playable by beginning recorder students. And finally we depart from the ubiquitous 2/4, 4/4 and 6/8 to a setting in 3/4, not an easy task using Mother Goose texts. This arrangement captures the genius of elemental music— simple, uncluttered, but musically evocative.

### Teaching Suggestions

- Create a "sound carpet" of wind sounds, with voice and/or select instruments (twirling plastic tubes, autoharp strings, blowing across bottles, etc.). Recite text freely. Group with scarves moves as the wind, one child is the robin trying to fly against the wind or shivering in the tree branch, another group creates a barn with their bodies for robin to take shelter.
- Add octave drone on bass metallophone, swirling sounds on the other barred instruments and melody on solo recorder. When all sing the song, the robin heads for the "barn." At the end of the song, the children forming the barn become the wing gently covering the robin as the opening wind sounds return and fade away.

# Peter Piper

Where's the peck of pick-led pep-pers Pe-ter Pi-per picked?

Pe-ter Pi-per picked a peck of pick-led pur-ple-pep-pers. Did

Pe-ter Pi-per pick a peck of pick-led pur-ple-pep-pers? If

Pe-ter Pi-per picked a peck of pick-led pur-ple pep-pers,

Where's the peck of pick-led pep-pers Pe-ter Pi-per picked?

## 32. PETER PIPER: Pentatonic transposition, kinesthetic learning, pick-ups and more tongue twisting

This is an exciting moment in the developmental sequence, when the children (3rd graders in my school) are introduced to the wonders of transposition. I believe that transposition is one of the "super- foods" in the music education diet, building strong musical minds 12 different ways—C, D♭, D, E♭, etc. (though here the children begin with a bite-size portion—C, F, and G). The ability to transpose clearly shows understanding of scales and melodies as a system of relationships. These first steps in transposing on Orff instruments are built for success—you can take the bars off to create the new pentatonic scales and still use the same sticking pattern.

We're back in the world of tongue twisters here, this one rife with p's (keep your distance from those juicy plosives!). You might set the mood for the piece by experimenting with P sounds and then play the opening of the Papageno-Papagena duet from Mozart's *Magic Flute*. This is also a great rhyme to perform with Keith Terry patterns, canon, augment/diminish, all those effective speech devices set forth in Part I.

The more common version of the poem (and one worth trying) features seven beat phrases in the first three lines. However, when one of my students said the version she knew was "pickled_purple peppers," it was hard to resist moving to the more comfortable eight beat phrase. We did, and this is the result.

### Teaching Suggestions

With instruments set in C pentatonic, play the melody and ask students to listen for a repeating pattern. When they hear that the first four notes of each phrase are the same, invite them to play along with right hand mallet only. While they play, ask them to listen for the ending patterns and as above, join in. Practice the entire melody and ask for a "thumbs evaluation" (thumbs up: great/ 45°:pretty good/ horizontal: so-so, etc.). Those with less than thumbs up must say what they didn't like (big intervals, boring rhythm, drone missing, etc.). Have them create a drone. Try out La and Do and then evaluate.

Some might think the ending sounds funny in La mode and some might think that A in the melody doesn't fit so well in the Do mode. Many will like both and some may suggest starting in La for the first part and ending in Do.

Ask students to guess why they played with right hand alone (when they've always been told to play with both hands) and then reveal that the left hand plays an eighth note "pivot" between each right hand note. The pivot on the G makes it more interesting to hear and more intriguing to play (play them Schumann's *Humming Song* and the Minuet from Bach's *Partita No. I*, BWV 825). Now review the drone accompaniments above and C will certainly come out as the proper choice.

Next play the double eighth notes at the end of each phrase and ask students to describe what was different. Again, with the pick-ups in the second and third phrases. Make sure they learn the term "pick-up"(you can relate it to Peter picking the peppers). Add the moving drone in the bass and off they go. For more excitement, begin slowly and increase the tempo at each repetition.

In the next class, review the piece; give the following problem:

> "F is the new Do. What notes would you take off to make this pentatonic scale? What note would you start on? Try playing the song." All play in F.

> "Now G is the new Do. Find that pentatonic and figure out what the problem is as you practice the song. (Most Orff instruments don't have high B—strike wooden trim piece instead)." All play in G.

> "Are you ready for the final exam? Try playing Peter Piper in C, F and G pentatonic, one after another, but now with all bars on. Good luck!"

If they succeed (an easy tempo helps), make it more challenging by:

1) Increasing the tempo
2) Playing in canon
3) Playing on the other side of the xylophone (like the teacher when modeling)
4) Playing with eyes closed

Then pick everyone up off the floor after they collapse in hilarious frustration.

## Extensions

- Add moving drone and try in canon.
- While teaching in Spain, I found the following tongue twister (*trabalengua*) and adapted it to the melody, extending the end of the phrase. It works!

> Cocodrillo come coco muy tranquilo poco a poco *
> Muy tranquilo poco a poco cocodrillo come coco
> Poco a poco muy tranquilo come coco cocodrillo
> Come coco cocodrillo coco come como no!

---

\* The crocodile eats coconut very calmly little by little.

The joy of Orff Schulwerk.

# Puss Came Dancing

Puss came danc-ing out of a barn, with a

pair of bag-pipes un-der her arm.

She could sing no-thing but "fid-dle cum fee, the mouse has mar-ried the

hum - ble - bee." Pipe, cat! Dance, mouse!

We'll have a wed-ding at our good house.

### 33. PUSS CAME DANCING: F Pentatonic, through composed, dance and an unlikely marriage

Prepared by Peter Piper for the pleasures of F pentatonic, the way is paved for Puss to prance out to the pasture with his pipes. Note that the 5th of the drone can now be played both above and below the tonic note F in a pleasing kinesthetic pattern. Likewise, the melody can dip below (as it does here), making F a necessary choice for singing (it would be too low for the children's voices in the key of C). Besides building musical muscle through transposition, here we hit on one of the primary functions of transposition—to set a comfortable key for the voice.

This arrangement differs from many of the previous ones in several important ways. Though the drone is still a foundation, it changes frequently here, offers a more challenging rhythm, drops out altogether and shifts to a pedal point on the 5th.

The melody is divided into call and response format, first answered by the woodblock (snare drum also works well here), then the instruments simulating the bagpipe drone, and then various comments by the other instruments. This arrangement is "through composed," meaning that there are no literal repeats in any of the parts. It demands more time and attention, but is a challenge worthy of the children's growing sophistication.

The text begs for a dance and both the words and the form suggest specific actions.

Here is a sample dance:

### A section: Two lines facing each other. All sing, accompanied by Orff instruments.

- "Puss" comes dancing down the middle following text. "Mouse" and "Humblebee" are standing at the other end in wedding pose; Puss dances around them.
- At "Pipe cat" and "Dance mouse," each responds accordingly.
- When the glockenspiel plays, quickly change two lines to one big circle with Puss, mouse and humblebee in the center.

### A$^1$: No singing, with alto and soprano xylophones playing the melody.

- Circle moves eight steps to the right, with mouse doing a solo fancy step on the woodblock part.
- Then eight steps to the left, with the humblebee soloing on the "bagpipe drones."
- On "pipe cat," all stay in place and clap three times; "Dance mouse," stamp three times.
- Turn around in place on last phrase. Take three steps in at glock entrance and shout "Hey!"

### A$^2$: Singing and playing together.

- All dance freely around room and stop to toast bride and groom with woodblock.
- Dance again and eat some wedding cake with "bagpipe" drones.
- Dance freely again.
- Stop at "pipe cat," clap three times and stamp three times as above.
- Toast in dramatic shape on final "Hey!"

Needless to say, there will be a lot of giggling about the marriage of the chosen mouse and humblebee. You may have to monitor the teasing, but the kids will secretly be delighted.

# This Is the House That Jack Built

This is the house that Jack built.

This is the malt that lay in the house that Jack built.

This is the rat that ate the malt, that

## 34. THE HOUSE THAT JACK BUILT—G pentatonic, 6/8, cumulative form, group composition and an intriguing chain of characters

This tour de force is actually simpler than it appears. Its complexity lies in the cumulative form of the text, one of many in this style (*There's a Hole in the Bottom of the Sea, The Rattlin' Bog*, etc.). The poem suggests an elaborate treatment and here it is: art, drama, movement, language, math and composition with percussion, Orff instruments and recorder. Between its cumulative form, irregular phrases, internal rhymes, alliteration (*tattered and torn, shaven and shorn*), colorful imagery (*a cow with a crumpled horn*) and sequential action, this rhyme is a miniature masterpiece. In addition to being a wonderful memory exercise, the relationships between the characters provide a springboard for discussion about the food chain, ecology, and interdependence.

I have two memories of this poem, the first from my 3rd grade class of 1995, whose collective composition I feature here. Because of the alliteration, I tried to do the original version of the rhyme and use the line "the cock that crowed in the morn." When the boys started giggling, I knew I had to change it to "rooster." But Pierce, a charming innocent boy, looked puzzled and asked why. I turned it over to the boys and when one of them said, "Because cock means penis," Pierce grimaced as if struck and said, "Aw! I wish you hadn't told me that!"

A less humorous, but more mystical moment occurred in one of my Orff teacher-training courses. We were casting the characters and had arrived at, "Who wants to be the priest all shaven and shorn?" At that instant, one of the students walked in late. Everyone looked wide-eyed in wonder—he had just shaved his head! When we explained what we were doing and why we were so astounded, it was his turn to look amazed. "Last night, I needed a poem for my homework assignment, so I called my friend who has a book of nursery rhymes. She decided she would choose for me by closing her eyes, opening the book and putting her finger randomly on the page—and the poem it landed on was *The House that Jack Built!*" We sang the theme from "The Twilight Zone," and proceeded to put on a marvelous production.

### Teaching Suggestions
+ Write key nouns from the rhyme on the board: *House, Jack, malt, rat, cat, dog, cow, maiden, man, priest, rooster, farmer*. Recite all nouns as if introducing a cast of characters, with students making shapes for each.
+ Write the verbs: *Built, lay, ate, killed, worried, tossed, milked, kissed, married, crowed, woke, sowed, fed*. Students silently make motions for each in turn (a 6/8 figure played on a drum helps frame the movements). Emphasize the "no touching" rule, especially for "killed!"
+ Have them begin to put the poem together, associating verbs with nouns. (You can give the first two lines as a model).
+ Write the adjectives on the board: *crumpled, forlorn, tattered and torn, shaven and shorn*; students associate them with their corresponding character.
+ All recite entire poem. Note change in form of last two verses—two nouns, two verbs.
+ Recite entire poem again, leaving eight beats after each line for students to mime the new action. Here you might note the irregular form of the first five verses. The first line is a comfortable four beats long, but the combination of line one and two is six. Line three (continuing to the beginning) is eight, line four is ten, line five is twelve. From here to the end, everything proceeds in multiples of four.
+ Divide into two groups of eleven each. (Adjust according to your class size, doubling kids on parts as necessary). Each student in the first group chooses a verse and draws a picture on a large piece of paper. Display the pictures in order on the wall for the graphic score.

Each then practices speaking their part and miming the action. Once they come in on their part, they continue speaking all subsequent parts, as follows:

1) "This is the house that Jack built."

2) "This is the malt that lay in the" (1&2) " house that Jack built."

3) This is the rat that ate the (2&3) malt that lay in the (1, 2 & 3) "house that Jack built." etc.

- Students in the second group choose a verse and an instrument to either play the part given in the score or create their own ostinato in 6/8. Begin with a drone in the bass to establish the beat then mix melodic ostinati on the barred instruments with unpitched percussion. For original ostinati, students must improvise in the order of the verses so that they have to listen to what precedes and complement that by filling in the appropriate spaces. Once an ostinato enters, it continues for the rest of the piece.
- Combine groups and perform.

# Advanced Arrangements—3rd to 5th Grade
Transposed pentatonic modes; major/minor modes;
shifting meters

Around 4th grade in my school, we come to the end of our introduction to the pentatonic scale and begin to enter new territory—the diatonic modes. Like teeth that have finally grown in, we fill the gap between E and G and play both pentachordal melodies (from C to G) and hexatonic melodies (from C to A) before arriving at the full diatonic scale from C to shining C. Most students will recognize this as the major scale, yet in Orff practice, it is something quite distinct—the Ionian mode. The Ionian mode and the major scale share the same seven notes, but have markedly different functions, the former still accompanied by drones, the latter by a complex system of chords.

By exploring the modes before functional harmony, students can continue from the base of familiar elemental orchestration and compose and improvise as they did in pentatonic, but now with two additional tones. Instead of Re or La mode, we can now use formal terminology recognized in Western theory classes—Ionian, Dorian, Phrygian and so on.

I have chosen not to include this modal study here. Though certainly possible to make modal arrangements of nursery rhymes and poetry, I tend to go to folk material and medieval music for repertoire (some of which I hope to share in a future book). By limiting this study to the pentatonic, we can experience its versatility and understand its role in Orff practice.

Included in the first part of this section are yet more integrated performances, tongue twisters and nonsense speech, a new concept (modal transposition), intriguing animals, a freely metered poem, more jazz mixed with a name game, multiple languages, English history, a challenging 9/8 meter and some simple melodies for the recorder. The final pieces are reserved for 5th grade, featuring transposed meters, polymeters and bi-tonality, diatonic modes over pentatonic accompaniment, alto recorder and the role of music in ritual. We end with two complex integrated performances, the last involving all five grades that summarizes just about everything covered in the book.

# Yes Sir, No Sir

3. Why do you speak so bold, Sir? Because I have a cold, Sir.
   Where did you get your cold, Sir? Up at the North Pole, Sir.
4. Where do you go to church, Sir? Down by yonder birch, Sir.
   Perhaps we then shall meet, Sir. If I rest my feet, Sir.

## 35. YES SIR NO SIR—Another integrated performance, more moving drones, prohibition and the radical roots of art

At one of my Orff workshops, someone asked if I really was allowed to do this song in my school. Puzzled, I asked, "Why not?" "Because you're singing about beer." The thinking seemed to be that if you sing a song that has the word beer in it, every child singing it will grow up to be an alcoholic.

I replied, "Do you remember 'The worms crawl in, the worms crawl out, the worms play pinochle on your snout?' 'My mother and your mother were hanging out clothes. My mother punched your mother right in the nose?' That chant we exuberantly shouted each June—'No more homework, no more books, no more teacher's dirty looks?' or 'Glory, glory, hallelujah, Teacher hit me with a ruler...?' Did those rhymes turn you into a morbid, violent or disrespectful person?"

As nursery rhyme collector Iona Opie, comments in *I Saw Esau: The Schoolchild's Pocket Book*,

> "These are not rhymes that a grandmother might sing to a grandchild on her knee. They have more oomph and zoom; they pack a punch. Many are directly concerned with the exigencies of school life; the need for a stinging reply when verbally attacked; the need for comic complaints in the face of persecution or the grinding drudgery of schoolwork; the need to know some clever rhymes by heart, with which to win popularity. They pass from one child to another without adult interference."

Yes, indeed. And even grandmother's nursery rhymes contain some hard themes; the little ditty about the Black Plague we know as *Ring Around the Rosy*, the three blind mice who get their tails chopped off, the man who confines his wife to a pumpkin shell and that strangest of all juxtapositions, the comforting melody of *Rock-a- bye Baby* with its terrifying climax.

I found the "beer" rhyme in a marvelous book *Skipping Around the World: The Ritual Nature of Folk Rhymes* by Francelia Butler, who echoes Opie's words:

> "In these rhymes, children can relieve pain by chanting their need for romance and identity, respond to the mysteries of life, protest real or imagined injustices and even cruelties inflicted by adults and adult world, compensate for loneliness, and above all, dream of a happy and self-determined future."

In other words, these rhymes are more than whimsical phonetic fluff. They serve the function of art, saying out loud that which is often suppressed, either by the ruling authorities or our own discomfort with facing life's gritty realities. When I encounter that Puritanical mindset of protecting children from a word like beer, I ask people to reflect on the stories found in the Bible, Greek myths and Shakespeare. Indeed, art, literature, myths, fairy tales and spiritual stories all suggest that we must pass through the vale of suffering, human cruelty and evil to fully and authentically taste joy and redemption. Art gives a shape and meaning to our suffering, transforming it through the humor of a rhyme, the beauty of a song or the resolution of a tale. It gives kids the tools to grapple with life's hard issues and to *"dream of a happy and self-determined future."*

By contrast, there is the meaningless and sensational roaring river of random violence that the media throws at us all daily, with children increasingly unprotected from the assault and rarely guided by an adult as they watch alone in their room. When parents complain about songs like this, I encourage teachers to counter with, "Does your child play video games? Read Cosmopolitan? Watch the 6 o'clock news? Know how to spell 'porn' and use Google? After we have that discussion, then let's talk about the word 'beer.'" *

After all that, we discover that *Yes Sir, No Sir* isn't about beer at all. It's a genre of rhyme that asks a question to gain power over another, a kind of Rumpelstiltskin interrogation like our rhyme "What's your name? Puddin' Tane. Ask me again and I'll tell you the same." I love the question/answer form, the re-occurrence of "Sir" (a word rarely spoken by the children I know), the exuberance of the driving accompaniment (good for 3rd graders) and the clear form of the dance followed by the exciting chaos of the free skipping. This also qualifies as a genuine integrated performance, bringing together as it does

---

\* For music teachers who don't want to go through all this, I simply suggest, "Change it to 'root beer.'"

song, dance, body percussion, Orff instruments and unpitched percussion. The "story" is whimsical and anti-narrative, with little or no connection between verses. Below is a dance and suggested form.

Divide singers into two lines facing each other and teach the following dance:
- Line 1 (questions): Four steps to the center.
- Line 2 (answers): Four steps to the center.
- Line 1: Four steps back to place.
- Line 2: Four steps back to place.
- Both lines: Perform body percussion in place.
- Both lines: 16 beats of free movement (skipping) around the space, back in place ready for next verse by the end.

**Form:**
8 beat instrumental intro., group one begins verse.
16 beat interlude on percussion (while dancers skip around the room).
8 beat intro. on Orff instruments, continue to next verse.
After last percussion interlude, all sing a final refrain.

3rd grade dancers.

# Two Tutors

all!

### 36. TWO TUTORS—Tongue-twisting limerick, color hocket, canon and a deep question

The limerick doesn't come to us from Limerick, Ireland, as I gleefully supposed when I once drove through that town. There are hints of this form as far back as the 13th century and the well-known rhyme *Hickory Dickory Dock*, first printed in 1744, has some characteristics of the limerick form. But it was the English poet Edward Lear who brought the form into its present day popularity with his *A Book of Nonsense* in 1845. Lear's poems firmly established a 6/8 meter with an A A b b A rhyming form, the first line often beginning "There was a…" and, in Lear's version, repeating in a slightly altered form in the last line:

> There was an Old Man of Kilkenny,
> Who never had more than a penny;
> He spent all that money,
> In onions and honey,
> That wayward Old Man of Kilkenny.

In other (and for me, more satisfying) examples, the last line is the punch line.

> A lively young damsel from Mingus
> Inquired, "Do you know what this thing is?"
> Her aunt, with a gasp,
> Replied, "It's a wasp,
> And you're holding the end where the sting is!"

One good way to learn about the form is to get it wrong.

> There was a young man from Japan
> Whose limericks never would scan.
> When asked why this was,
> He answered "because
> I always try to fit as many syllables into the last line as ever possibly I can."

> Vincent Van Gogh couldn't hear.
> Because he had only one ear.
> When asked to reply,
> He said with a sigh,
> "Eh?"

When I teach limericks at workshops and ask the teachers if they know any, I always add, "that are appropriate to share." Some sources speculate that bawdy limericks were popular in the tavern (perhaps in Limerick?) and cleaned up later by Lear and his successors. This anonymous limerick supports the ribald history:

> The limerick packs laughs anatomical
> In space that is quite economical,
> But the good ones I've seen
> So seldom are clean,
> And the clean ones so seldom are comical.

Two Tutors is doubly delicious because it combines the tongue-twister with the limerick. Two others in this genre, the first by Ogden Nash:

> A flea and a fly in a flue
> Were imprisoned, so what could they do?
> Said the fly, "Let us flee!"
> "Let us fly!" said the flea
> So they flew through a flaw in the flue.

> A canner exceedingly canny
> One morning remarked to his granny.
> "A canner can can
> Anything that he can
> But a canner can't can a can, can he?"

And finally, one more very clever one, source unknown:

She frowned and called him Mr.
Because in sport, he Kr.
And so in spite,
That very night,
This Mr. Kr. Sr. *

Our treatment of this limerick should feel quite familiar, returning us to the "say, play, say and play" model, the use of the color part and the always-exciting canon. However, a few little noteworthy twists make this lesson even more interesting for the children:

1) The two-note color part on recorder creates a little hocket melody.
2) The echo section at the end of the canon.
3) The question: "Is it easier to play the flute or teach it?"
4) Investigating the above question. Have the children volunteer in pairs (two tutors) to be either "students," "teachers," or "musicians" (of course, we know that music teachers need to be all three!) The students are those who had trouble with the echo section, the teachers those who were comfortable with it and the musicians those who found it quite easy. Two teachers pair up with two students and try to teach them the echoed patterns plus the next part on the second line in the arrangement that follows. Two musicians go off and either read the music on the top line or learn from the adult teacher. At the end, all sections join to play *Edi Beo*, a medieval song.

## Edi Beo

Old English

---

\* Mr. Kr. Sr. = Mister kissed her sister.

Two tutors tooting recorders.

# Donkey Donkey

## 37. DONKEY DONKEY—Transposed Sol mode and the gentility of elders

This donkey, softened and wise with age, doesn't brashly hee and haw, but gently brays to wake the world on a sleepy morn. And so this tender arrangement, playable by 4th graders on recorder and easy on the ears with the sonorous blend of Orff instruments.

The Sol mode, like Mi, is rarely found in folk literature. Unlike the Mi mode, the 5th is available for the drone, but most melodies starting or ending on Sol tend to be plagal versions of Do and don't feel coherently supported by this drone. In this arrangement, I make every effort to anchor the 5th both in the melody and in the accompaniment, but it still wouldn't be a surprise to end the whole affair on the Do. In any case, it gives the arrangement a different flavor and appropriately so, as the aging donkey is indeed somewhat apart from the crowd.

In the key of C, this would either be too low or too high for the children's voices and hence, this is an example of a transposed mode, set in G pentatonic.

This could be an interesting companion piece to *Little Boy Blue* waking the world with his horn. (You'll have to arrange that rhyme yourself.) Throw in a few rooster songs or rhymes and you have a "waking-the-world-fantasia" and many choices to integrate into drama. In all cases, begin with some dawn sounds improvised vocally by the children— quiet bird whistles, hearty rooster crows and gentle donkey brays.

# The Fog

"The fog comes
On little cat feet.
It sits
Looking over harbor and city
on silent haunches.
And then…
Moves on."

Recite poem in free meter above metered accompaniment. Stop accompaniment after "silent haunches,"
play last chord after "moves on."

## 38. THE FOG—Re mode, sound carpet and the beauty of language

Here we take a left turn from nursery rhymes into the poetry of Carl Sandburg and the weather of my hometown, San Francisco. It was here that I had one of the most aesthetically satisfying experiences in all my years of workshop teaching. It took place at the summer Orff certification course in a year when there was a particularly rich cornucopia of students who translated this poem into French, Spanish, Portuguese, Italian, Russian, German, Swedish, Hebrew, Farsi, Hindi, Bahasa Indonesian, Chinese, Vietnamese and Japanese! For the finale, they entered from different corners moving freely with scarves reciting the poem in their own language. The effect was mesmerizing, the languages overlapping like fog curling over the San Francisco hills. As the last words were spoken, the instrumental parts began and the poem was repeated in English as the speakers continued to move with their scarves, exiting on the phrase "moves on."

I have done this many times since and have never been disappointed. The sonic beauty of each language is framed by this setting, enhanced by the contrast with the music of other languages and the poetic intention of the text. As the voices overlap and the distinct sounds begin to blend, it is indeed like the swirl of the fog. Meanwhile, the Re mode, with no 3$^{rd}$ to define it as either major or minor, is the perfect background for the amorphous quality of fog. And the unmetered speech over the metered accompaniment creates a refreshing break from our beat-based four-phrase, metered settings. Don't forget to add sound-effects—both vocal and instrumental—at the beginning to set the mood.

This is an opportunity for children with English as a second language to share the beauty of their mother tongue. Let them translate the poem into their own language—it needn't be precisely correct. If more than one child speaks another language, let them work as a group. Naturally, it is fine to simply perform the poem in English.

Dancers with fans.

# Mama Lama Kuma Lama

### African-American Children's Chant

Ma - ma  la - ma  ku - ma  la - ma  ku - ma - la - bee - stay___

Oh  no - no  no_____  no  na - bee - stay

Ee - ny - mee - ny - gyp - sa - lee - ny  oo - ah - ah___  ma - lee - ny

Ot - chy  pot - chy  Li - be - ra - ce  who  are  you?___

Clap
Chest
Pat Thighs
Back of Thighs
Step
Clap
Chest
Pat Thighs
Back of Thighs
Step

- Teach both body percussion patterns above. Divide between partners.
- Echo text to *Mama Lama*; perform as clapping play with partner.
- One speaks: "My name is Kate," other responds "Ooh-ah!"
  "And I like to skate," other "ooh-ah!" Switch.
- Two lines of 12, facing about 15 feet apart.

## FORM:
  A) Body percussion parts moving towards each other.
  B) Clap play with partner singing song.
  C) Speak name to partner with "Ooh-ah!" response.
  D) Body percussion parts moving away while head couple struts down the middle to instrumental music. Four couples go, repeat all.

# Mama Lama

### 39. MAMA LAMA—Transposed La-mode, body percussion, walking bass, jazz improvisation and name rhyming

Here is yet another integrated performance, jazz-style. It starts from the kids' world of nonsense rhymes sung as a handjive and grows by adding body percussion, contra-dance formation, struttin' down the alley and jazz solos. We can never have too many models of this winning formula—bring the street game or playground chant into the sequenced pedagogy of formal—but still playful—musical development.

There are many variants of this text, but none of them end with "who are you?" I added that to create another name game for introducing people at the beginning of my workshops and classes.

The first part of the arrangement can be taught mostly without speaking, beginning with the body percussion and proceeding from there (I play piano for strutting down the aisle). Naturally, the process can be spread over many classes as each part— body percussion, clapping play, name rhyme, etc.—requires some attention.

Once again, it's worth teaching all the instrumental parts to everyone, beginning in the body and the voice. Then, with the instruments in a circle, invite one child to the first instrument to play the part assigned. On a cue, that child moves to the second instrument and another plays the first. Continue until all instruments are filled and then keep rotating around the circle until all have played everything. If there aren't enough instruments for every child, leave a space in-between each one where a child can sit and study the next part while waiting. At the end of the entire sequence (probably the next class), have children select parts they're comfortable with. In a big class, some play and some dance.

The first half of the instrumental arrangement can be played from the body percussion through the clapping play. When the head couples strut down the aisle, switch to the walking bass with melodic solos. Repeat whole sequence as needed.

*Mama Lama*, like *Old Man Mosie*, brings American rhymes with their jazz inflection into the mix. The body percussion is an exciting challenge for upper elementary students and helps them prepare to play the drum set. The name rhyme is a different kind of challenge, especially for some children's names. Sam was quite happy with the exercise. "My name is Sam. I like Green Eggs and Ham," but poor Ethan was less pleased. "My name is Ethan. I like…I can't think of anything!!" (big tears here). Later, he finally came up with "I like to eat Wheat Thins." Close enough! With difficult names, I suggest using a nickname or simply scat singing a response. (I once did this with 4th graders who never sang songs or recited rhymes in their school and was astounded at how hard it was for them to rhyme even the simplest names. Their lack of this essential foundation reaffirmed my belief in the importance of rhymes and songs in the school curriculum.)

The arrangement features a bass vamp that serves a drone-like function and a minor pentatonic scale that gives it a blues feeling. The "ooh-ah" echoes two chords used in the well-known Miles Davis' tune "*So What*" and the children get their first taste of a simple walking bass. The call and response form is maintained in the improvisation. Don't forget to swing it!

# Humpty Dumpty

## IV. Lament for Humpty—Slow and Mournful

Oh no no. oh no no. Hump-ty's gone we'll miss him

Oh no no. oh no no. Hump-ty's gone we'll miss him so.

## V. Grand Finale—Resume First Tempo

Oh no no. Oh no no.

so.

## 40. HUMPTY DUMPTY—Transposed La mode in G, 6/8, the suite and the mystery of the egg

Many compositions arise from particular needs—Bach composes another chorale for the Sunday church service, Richard Rodgers writes the next song for a Broadway show or Tito Puente gets a tune ready for next Saturday night's dance. So do Orff teachers, who sometime create pieces that come from the students' needs. This arrangement grew out of *Lament for Humpty*, a simple round I wrote for beginning recorder students.

Departing from the ABA or rondo form so common in Orff arrangements, we are here trying to illuminate each section of the poem in the manner of a suite, with its varying tempos and shades of feeling. The La mode of G pentatonic featured here is a friendly scale for the beginning soprano recorder player. Rhythmically, we're back in 6/8, following the natural meter of the poem.

Why do we think Humpty is an egg? The original poem is a riddle, but as nursery rhymes found their way into books, the punch line was stolen by the illustrators, planting the image in our minds. Robert Carter, in his book *The Tao and Mother Goose*, speculates that Humpty (including its various versions in French and Swedish) is one of the oldest rhymes we know and refers to the Cosmic Egg, our divine wholeness before we enter the realm of time and space, fall from Paradise and are broken. Trying to restore wholeness through will and ego will not work—we simply, in Buddhist fashion, need to realize our Original Nature. Other less cosmic interpretations link Humpty to a broken cannon and Richard III. Humpty also makes a guest appearance in Lewis Carroll's *Through the Looking Glass*.

# Hickety Pickety

## 41. HICKETY PICKETY—Major/ minor, canon, hemiola and a Latin hen

This arrangement came from a pedagogical purpose—a review of the first four notes my 3<sup>rd</sup> graders learn on the soprano recorder. It also demonstrates that a piece need not be wholly major or wholly minor, but can swing back and forth (Do and La pentatonic in this example). The piece should be alternately sung and played, in unison and in canon (enter at each measure).

A second section varies the tune by alternating 6/8 and 3/4 meter. This rhythmic device, called hemiola, is found throughout much Latin American music and is most popularly known in Leonard Bernstein's song from *West Side Story*— "**I** wan-na **live** in A-/ **mer-i-ca**." To dramatize the song, have half the group play and half do a chicken dance, showing the hemiola accents with their necks.

First graders gently passing around a black hen.

# The Lion and the Unicorn

The li - on and the u - ni-corn were fight-ing for the crown.____ The li - on beat the

## 42. THE LION AND THE UNICORN—Minor-Major, 6/8—2/4, and the impossible tangles of English history

This is the third in a series written for beginning soprano recorder. Whereas *Hickety Pickety* moved from major to minor, this arrangement goes from minor to major and also features a metrical shift. The form is simple—sing once, play once, then sing and play together. Feel free to add melodic improvisation.

King James VI of Scotland was the son of Mary, Queen of Scots and began his reign at one year old in the year 1567. In 1603, he succeeded Elizabeth I of England, as she died without heir, and became James 1, ruling over England, Scotland and Ireland. As the Scottish coat of arms had two unicorns and the English, two lions, he combined the two on a new Coat of Arms. This is the story I found associated with this rhyme.

Yet contradictions abound. The rhyme says "The lion beat the unicorn," but nowhere in this story is any conflict mentioned. Furthermore, who gave white bread, brown bread and plum cake to whom? Who drummed whom out of town and why? In my research, I have not found anyone addressing these questions. Since the facts are obscure, let the kids use their imagination and write "The Untold Tale of the Lion and the Unicorn."

# Cock Robin

Soprano Recorder

Who killed Cock - Rob - in? Who killed Cock -

Glockenspiel

Alto Metallophone

Alto Metallophone

Bass Metallophone

Bass Bars

SR

Rob - in? "It was I" said the spar - row "with my

Glock.

AM

AM

BM

BB

lit-tle bow and ar-row, it was I___ it__ was_ I."

2. Who saw him die-o? Who saw him die'o?
   "It was I, " said the Fly, "With my little teeny eye,
   It was I, it was I."
3. Who caught his blood'o? Who caught his blood'o?
   "It was I," said the Fish. "with my little silver dish,
   It was I, it was I."
4. "Who made the coffin?...
   "It was I," said the Snipe, "with my little pocket knife..."
5. Who made the shroud'o...
   "It was I," said the Beetle, "with my little thread and needle..."
6. Who dug the grave'o?...
   "It was I, " said the Crow, "with my little spade and hoe..."
7. Who lowered him down'o?...
   "It was I, " said the Crane, "with my little golden chain..."
8. Who sang the preachment?...
   "It was I," said the Rook, with my little holy book..."

## 43. COCK ROBIN—Tranposed La, folk song and the last rites of birds

This haunting melody is the only one in this collection that was not composed by me or the children—it is an English folk song. It was included in the first published collection of nursery rhymes, *Tommy Thumb's Pretty Song Book*, published in 1744. Just how and when it changed from rhyme to song is not known. Some suggest that the text is a veiled reference to Robin Hood, others associate it with the political decline and fall of Sir Robert Walpole, minister to King George II in England, in 1742. *The Annotated Mother Goose* suggests that it may be related to a more ancient Norse myth about the slaying of Balder and others have tried to link it to the ritual killing of the wren on St. Stephen's Day in England.

Interesting as these speculations may be, it is this beautiful melody accompanied by the instruments that will touch the children. The power of music to evoke emotion at life's big events—be it joy at weddings or grief at funerals—is something that children should come to know. Through the mock funeral of a bird, the children are learning how to hold sadness in their hearts and express grief through beauty.

The images certainly lend themselves to movement and/or dramatic interpretation and this is an excellent chance to feature some solo singers, as well as talented recorder players.

Upper elementary singers.

# The Owl

A wise old owl sat in an oak.
The more he heard, the less he spoke.
The less he spoke, the more he heard.
Why can't we all be like that wise old bird?

## 44. THE OWL—Alto recorder and the wisdom of listening

This is yet another freely spoken poem over a metered setting. Begin with the bass and add each part one at a time after each of the first three spoken lines. After "The more he heard…," feel free to add more instruments—light percussion, sound effects, alto recorder improvisation, etc. On cue, all stop and recite line and then play final chord.

By now, you and your upper elementary children will have your own ideas about how to develop and perform this poem. Following the owl's advice, I'll refrain from further comments.

# Sally Go 'Round the Sun I—Kids' Version

## 45. SALLY GO 'ROUND THE SUN I— Shifting chords, student composition and the Orff Ensemble Carousel

I was hired to teach music at my school for one reason only— a parent had bought six Orff instruments and nobody knew what to do with them. I had taken one Orff class in college, so they hired me. That was in 1975, when both the Orff movement in the U.S. and I were just beginning our long climb up the slope of effective teaching practice. We had to rely on experimentation, exploration and just plain messin' around—some of my earlier classes were nothing more than pentatonic jam sessions. For all that this approach failed to accomplish, it did turn us back on our own aural resources and produced some inspired moments, of which this piece is an example.

As always, it feels right to layer the ostinati one at a time. Once the melody is in, it can be extended by an alto recorder rendition and then sung again. The end can either fade out or the instruments drop out one by one. The precision of the interlocking parts reminds me of a merry-go-round and with the theme of Sally circling and circling and the timbre of the instruments, it's a nice image to hold in mind. For a little dramatic interpretation, the musicians can be in the center facing out and the dancers revolving around them on the Orff Carousel.

Four decades of investigation and practice in the Orff movement has created a foundation of conceptual principles and effective practices that have saved many wheels from being re-invented. Yet sometimes such development starts to calcify into dogma and we start to distrust the value of the "jam session." This piece serves as a reminder to keep experimenting and exploring, set off on a trip to the moon not knowing how you're going to get there—and then see what happens.

# Sally Go 'Round the Sun II—Polymetric Version

Sal-ly go 'round the chim-ney pots. Ev' - ry af - ter - noon.

## 46. SALLY GO 'ROUND THE SUN II—Polymeter, diatonic mode and more complex orbits

Yet another version of Sally from those early experimental days, this features four different meters orbiting simultaneously and arriving once again at the beginning of this 60 beat cycle until they arrive at a point of unison 60 beats later. (Note how the four meters converge because 60 is divisible by 3, 4, 5 and 6.) The accompaniment is all pentatonic, but the melody suggests a Lydian mode (in C) played over the ostinati.

Here the upper elementary kids experience a more sophisticated use of ostinato typical of some minimalist compositions in the style of Steve Reich. This can be prepared and/or augmented with this body percussion exercise (all played simultaneously):

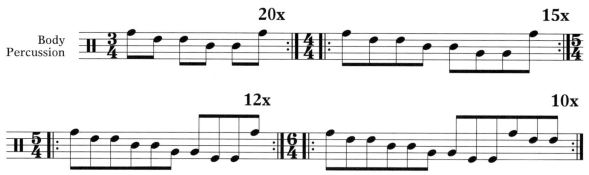

For further enhancement, punctuate the beginning of each meter with Tibetan cymbals, gongs or other ringing instruments (as suggested in *Davy Davy Dumpling*, bundt pans are wonderful). The players can add a visual effect by creating a gesture with their arms after striking their instrument. Both the aural and visual effect is mesmerizing.

# Sally Go 'Round the Sun—6/8 Game

noon.

Boom boom!

Ev' - ry af - ter-noon.

Boom boom!

chim - ney pots. Ev' - ry af - ter-noon.

Boom boom!

Sal-ly go 'round the chim - ney pots. Ev' - ry af - ter-noon.

Boom boom!

SALLY GO 'ROUND THE SUN

# Sally Go 'Round the Sun—3/4 Body Percussion

## Sally Go 'Round the Sun–4/4 Canon

## 47. SALLY GO 'ROUND THE SUN—Three modes, three keys, three meters and a ritual journey to outer and inner space

Fasten your seat belts—we're taking a ride beyond the horizon. These three versions of *Sally*, stitched into one event, both summarize key concepts and dynamic process and also take us into new territory far beyond the classroom. We've discussed musical, pedagogical, historical, cultural, and psychological meanings and now we're moving into the realm of myth.

Myths are the means by which we find our place in the cosmos, stories that help articulate and create our sense of meaning in an outwardly meaningless world. Every culture and religion has its defining myths that vary according to time, place and circumstance, but are alike in certain archetypal motifs—the trickster, the animal helpers, the hero's journey and more. These stories and images serve as guides for our inner life.

If myth is the story, ritual is the enactment of the story that drives the meaning deeper, connecting the imagination with the body and with a community of participants. Curt Sachs, a pioneering ethnologist, wrote in his groundbreaking book *World History of the Dance:*

> "In the ecstasy of the dance man bridges the chasm between this and the other world, to the realms of demons, spirits, and God. It represents a conscious effort to become a part of those powers beyond the might of man which control our destiny."

Carl Orff spent his life expressing these larger meanings through his art. His work defies categorization—neither music nor theater nor dance alone, but often a confluence of all three. His compositions drew from myths and fairy tales and performances of his works often have a ritualistic quality. It is little wonder that Orff's subsequent work in education is so well suited for creating child-size rituals and enacting myths through musical drama.

*Sally Go 'Round the Sun* offers a child-sized door into universal myths unencumbered by theology or dogma. The earth revolves around the sun, the moon orbits the earth, the earth spins on its own axis ("every afternoon") and one way to become "part of the powers which control our destiny" is for us to re-enact those circlings. The sun and moon are not only physical entities that control our survival and affect the tides and our moods, but also deep archetypal images that represent the principles of generation and reflection, hot and cool, light and dark, masculine and feminine.

And what of the chimney pots? (Some say chimney tops, evoking Sally as a kind of Peter Pan flying over the rooftops of London.) According to Wisegeek.com:

> "Chimney pots were traditionally unglazed pots with a tapered shape, designed to increase the draft of a chimney while providing an ornamental cap to a building."

Some associate it with the pot that sits on the hearth to collect the ashes. This is a potent image that evokes a cycle of time and calls to mind the phoenix that rises from the ashes. Stories of death, resurrection and the perpetual cycling of life abound in the world's mythology and Sally evokes all three. It was with these thoughts in mind that I created this three-part performance of Sally, one that children enjoy, but is especially evocative for adults. Though pedagogy should take a back seat to ritual in this event, taking one text through three different keys, modes and meters helps build our musical understanding and compositional skills as well.

**Teaching the Pieces**

**Part 1: The Dramatic Dying**

The original game in 6/8 is straightforward enough and one easily introduced in preschool. Something different has to happen on the "Boom! Boom!" and the typical choices are to change direction or fall down. (For a fun variant, change the quality of the circling and singing each time—slow, minor key, scary voice, etc.)

Our version here is performed in canon by four separate circles. Outside each circle is one person with a hand drum circling the other way. This person plays the "Boom! Boom!" over the head of whoever arrives at that moment, who then clutches his or her chest and falls down slowly in the kind of dramatic death young children specialize in. The circle keeps going in the same direction as people drop one by one (sometimes gently overlapping on the heap of bodies in the middle). When it becomes impossible to hold hands, simply keep circling. The rule of the game is that all players must maintain a walking beat at all times—no speeding up or slowing down to avoid the drum. The moral? When your time is up, it's up.

Note that this starting game is **Do pentatonic in F, 6/8 meter in a lively tempo.**

**Part II: Coming Back to Life**

The drummer, who was the bringer of bad tidings, now changes directions, reverses the drum mallet and becomes the bringer of life. Some instrumentalists begin playing the 3/4 version and the drummer taps one person during the glockenspiel part, who slowly rises and performs one of the body percussion patterns in the score. At the end of this process, all are performing one of the three patterns around the room while heading toward a pre-assigned circle. Alternate between singing the song twice and playing it on recorders twice. Recorder players may also try some improvised sections.

All of this naturally needs to be prepared ahead of time. The first task is to transpose the text to 3/4. Have the children conduct in 3 and recite the rhyme. The trick is to maintain the integrity of the strong beats. In 6/8, the syllable "Sal" is the downbeat of the first measure and the word "sun" is the downbeat of the second measure—in 3/4, the same must hold true. (See score for one of several correct answers.)

Then comes the melody, first sung and then played on recorder. Teach supporting parts and practice the body percussion, eventually letting children choose the pattern they're most comfortable with. Once all of this is in place, they are ready to perform as above.

Note that Part II is the **La mode of G pentatonic, 3/4 meter at a medium tempo.**

**Part III: The Continuity of Life**

Following the above metrical exercise, have the children transfer the text to 4/4 meter. Sing the melody using Curwen handsigns while walking in a circle, one step every two beats. Sing the melody once to the right, once to the left and once facing center. One student or teacher in the center of the circle can play the ostinato on two timpani (or a large frame drum) and a cymbal, symbolic of the sun and moon.

Form four concentric circles around the percussion player, circles 1 and 3 facing right, 2 and 4 facing left. Sing from inside to outside in four part canon, entering every two beats and circling as indicated. Hold the last note the third time through until all are joined in unison and end on the next cymbal stroke.

This canon features the interval of the second and the concentric circles going in opposite directions create a magical effect as the word "round" keeps passing by the singers.

Note that Part III is in **Do pentatonic in C, 4/4/ meter at a slow tempo.**

# Intery Mintery

### 48. INTERY MINTERY—Cross-grade collaboration, Re pentatonic and Dorian mode, organum, Bulgarian bagpipes and the ultimate-ritual-cross-grade-integrated-performance!

If our cosmic *Sally Go 'Round the Sun* ritual may seem a bit abstract for kids, this one hits them right where they live—in the fantastic world of Halloween. Often before the first day of school is out, some kids are already asking, "When are we going to practice *Intery Mintery?*"

We have many ceremonies and rituals at our school that are specific to us (see *Play, Sing and Dance*), but because Halloween is part of our mainstream culture, this one is especially delightful for the kids. This Mother Goose counting-out rhyme is not normally connected with Halloween, but the mystical text with its potent archetypal images of apples, seeds, thorns, twisting briars, flocking geese and water-springs makes it a natural fit.

Repetition is part of what gives ritual its power and we have celebrated with *Intery Mintery* for over 25 years. But good ritual, like good art, is also a perpetual work-in-progress and every year, we (the children, my colleagues James Harding and Sofía López-Ibor and I) add an idea here or refine a detail there. It just keeps getting better.

*Intery Mintery* is the most comprehensive and complex of the integrated performances offered here and as you work with it, you will see why it deserves the book's title. It involves five elementary grades, combines speech, song, percussion, Orff instruments, recorders, movement, folk dance and drama. The children experience the whole developmental arch in one big gulp. And all from a simple nursery rhyme.

### Teaching Suggestions

This will take a lot of preparation—that is, until it becomes an annual event. Then the alert children already know what's in store for them the following year— many learn their next grade's part simply by listening and watching. Before settling into their given role, all grades will learn the chant, the song (in canon and parallel 5ths), the motions to the song, and the dance.

James helped create the song's motions, as follows:

1st phrase—pat rhythm of text on knees

2nd phrase—fingers closed descending like pulling a thread, open to a "claw" on "thorn"

3rd phrase—crossing, twisted rising arms, loud clap over the head on "lock"

4th phrase—spread hands, touch thumbs and make flying motion

5th phrase—hands lower to rhythm in air, move side to side like a flowing spring

6th phrase—lean back and then in again

An overview of each grade's contribution is as follows:

### First Grade: Sound effects

The story starts at midnight on All Hallow's Eve and first grade is responsible for setting a mysterious mood with spooky sound effects. This is the time to dig deep into the percussion box for all those unusual instruments. Or play a more common one in new ways—fingernails scratching the head of a drum, brushes tickling a large cymbal, a ratchet slowly turning. An autoharp with each string plucked one at a time is quite effective, as are piano strings struck with a mallet inside of the piano. One student will ring a gong to mark the 12 strokes of the clock.

In the class, children experiment to create an unmetered "sound carpet." The challenge is to leave enough silence to frame each sound and not overly clutter the aural space. To this end, I sometimes give the kids "sound allowances" —each gets three sounds and they decide when to "spend" them. In performance, each instrument is assigned a particular stroke of the clock.

## Second Grade: Hocket melody, jack o'lantern faces and black light fans

In this one developed by Sofía, half of the second grade plays the melody hocket style using Boom-whackers, individual chime bars or angklung (Indonesian bamboo rattles). We encountered various hocket versions of text in Part I of this book, but now the kids have to follow the exact contour of the melody, playing their note only at the right time in the sequence. This is a perfect challenge for 2nd grade and a fascinating way to assess how well they have internalized the melody. At the beginning of the process, I see how much they can figure out on their own. As an intermediate step, I conduct—they play when I point to them. Sometimes I have a child conduct. The ultimate goal is for them to be independent and after a few practice sessions, they are.

The other half of the class sits behind a black light with specially painted fans (use Glow-in-the-Dark phosphorescent paint) held in front of their faces. At the end of each phrase, they take the fans away and make a face. We choreograph a sequence with six different jack o'lantern faces (surprised, scary, silly, scared, mad and a face of their choice) and six different ways to take away the fans (up, down, left, right, etc.).

## Third Grade: Orff instrument ensemble

Third grade plays the arrangement as written, minus the recorder part. All the parts are simple, but they must be sustained over a long time. You can use part of the text to teach each part: Glock= "Five geese" / SX= "Apple seed, apple thorn" / AX = "Intery Mintery" (divide the four notes amongst two players). No instrument plays the melody.

James recently added yet another brilliant touch—playing the instruments with glow-in-the-dark pens that have a little rubber ball at the end. It's quite magical to *see* the patterns as well as hear them!

## Fourth Grade: The Dance

This is the centerpiece of the entire performance, beginning with bodies awakening one part at a time (see below for details) and eventually dancing freely through space. Because we perform this on Halloween, the kids are in costume and move according to their character. The movement has a simple focus—following the contra bass pattern, move during three slow beats and take a scary contrasting shape on the cymbal. To help focus the movement yet further, I divide the group in half (generally, girls and boys is the easiest) and half dance while half are frozen. I encourage the moving group to think of prepositions while moving amidst the frozen shapes—around, over, under, through. They move for the length of the text, then switch. After each group has performed, all move and reveal their contrasting shape to the other participants seated around the room.

This is a great time to review all the principles of creative movement—time, space and energy. Encourage the kids to vary their tempos—fast, medium, slow, changing between different tempos. Remind them to use all the space—think high levels, low levels. side to side as well as forward and back. Check the energy of their movement—does it have a sharp focus, an extra sense of alertness in the body, a full commitment? Though the metered music is playing, they needn't move to the beat as the free movement makes an exciting counterpoint.

In the midst of this swirling motion, I play a new melody on the gaida, a Bulgarian bagpipe. This is an instrument I fell in love with and have integrated into the event. It's unlikely you will include the gaida, so feel free to substitute accordion, clarinet, violin, etc., played by a student or an adult. The 12-measure *Intery* and the 16 measure *Rada Pere* create an interesting polyrhythmic tension, meeting at 48 measures (*Intery* played four times, *Rada Pere* three times).

# Rada Pere

Macedonia

When the dancers hear this melody, they form a circle and perform this dance.

**A SECTION:** Grapevine step (cross-side-back-side) beginning crossing right foot over left and moving to the left. Dip body down on the cross and back steps.

**B SECTION:** Three steps toward center, light bounce with left foot raised on 4th beat, three steps back and close feet together. Repeat.

### Fifth Grade: Soprano and Alto Recorders

For fifth grade, the celebration provides the perfect motivation to begin alto recorder. They begin by learning the melody on soprano recorder starting on A (see score). They then play the same fingering on the alto, effortlessly creating parallel 5ths, a powerful effect known as *organum*. Some can also try the tenor, bass and sopranino recorder with the same fingering.

### THE SETTING:

1st grade: stage right with sound effect instruments
2nd grade: stage left with chime bars, angklung, painted fans and black light, in 4 rows
3rd grade: seated upstage left/center at Orff instruments
4th grade: lying in a circle with arms crossed and heads to center
5th grade: seated with recorders upstage right/center

> **NARRATOR:** Once a year, on All Hallow's Eve, it is said that the veil between the land of the dead and the land of the living grows very thin. For one glorious night, the dead, who have been lying cold and stiff all year in the ground, can once more cross back to the world of the living and make merry mischief. So when the sun sets in the west, little sounds can be heard in the forest.—(1st graders). And when the clock begins to chime 12, little whispers are heard to awaken the dead—(all) On the second chime, the fingers of the dead begin to move— (selected sound effects accompany each chime). On the third chime, the nose starts to wiggle. On the 4th, the mouth begins to chew. On the 5th, the eyes pop open. On the 6th, the toes begin to wiggle, on the 7th legs begin to shiver. On the 8th, the head rolls from side to side and on the 9th the arms begin to rise. On the 10th, the whole body shakes and on the 11th, it starts rising slowly. By the 12th, all the dead are seated (long sitting, facing out) and they begin to whisper their magic chant.

- 4th graders whisper Intery Mintery with motions, each at their own tempo and each suddenly taking hook sitting position at the end.
- 2nd grade plays melody hocket-style on angklung and chime bars while other 2nd graders cover faces with fans and brooms and reveal a scary face at the end of each phrase. During all of this, 4th graders do a slow half turn to face the center of the circle.
- 3rd grader enters with bass bar part. All sing song once, then in 4-part canon. 4th grade circle divided into quadrants, with one other grade singing with each quadrant.

- Alto recorders play while dancers rise. Alto and soprano (also bass and tenor) play while dancers move in place with motions of the song.
- All sing in parallel 5ths.
- 3rd grade enters—all parts at once— as teacher improvises on sopranino. Boy dancers freeze while girls move in and out, freezing at the end of each phrase. Switch. Recorders play again in 5ths and all move.
- Bagpipe (or accordion/ clarinet/ etc.) plays *Rada Pere* and dancers begin. After one cycle of the dance cyle, recorders join on *Intery* melody and play four times. Angklung rattle at the beginning of each phrase. All parts build to crescendo.
- Dancers stop and melt with sound effects. Six strokes of the gong to return to the graves with sound effects. Body parts stop wiggling one by one until all are still again, arms crossed.
- Narrator finishes: *And there they lie for one more year, until next* (pause) *All* (pause) *Hallow's* (pause) *Eve.*
- Final recorder chord. Dancers arms shoot up.

## A Musical Culture

Remember young James from our Preface? Soon after the class in which he breathlessly outlined the entire Halloween celebration, I began practicing it with the 4th grade. I noticed two 8th graders peeking in the window and doing the motions with us, looking a bit nostalgic. Later, I began working on the chant with the five-year-olds. I hardly had to teach the piece at all because some already knew it from older siblings—it was in the air, passed on from year to year, from kid to kid.

This is a glimpse into a musical culture larger than mere music education and grander than the private lessons. Here music is no longer a subject to be taught— it is a living part of the landscape, absorbed by the children and indelibly merged with their world. It spills out into recess, rises up as a song while painting in art class or a dance while waiting for their ride home. This vision of a musical culture was formed by my travels to Bali, Brazil, Bulgaria and beyond and one I was determined to bring to my school. *Intery Mintery* stands as a living example of those hopes realized, a celebration that gathers together everything I care about in music, culture and education.

Regularly scheduled music classes with grade-specific curriculums have their value, indeed, are vital in creating a musical culture. But the greater goal is to musicalize the whole community, to fill the school with celebrations and rituals, to let the sounds drift out the windows and entice the passer-bys to peek in. It comes from selecting memorable material for memorable occasions and presenting it in memorable ways. Not that children will always remember how they got from point A to point B, but that stored in the muscle memory of their hearts is a feeling of the place where they laughed, played, and sang their way into magical communion.

Seen from one point of view, *Intery Mintery* is a bit of Mother Goose fluff that has little to do with the kind of "academic excellence" and "preparation for success" that we often accept as the norm. But listening to James and watching those 8th grade girls and feeling the excitement in the room as the five-year- olds danced, I thought to myself:

"It doesn't get any better than this." Connection. Conviviality. Communion. Magic. Mystery. Music. The geese are flocking overhead, the spring is flowing and the children are sitting on the banks singing. Music in schools may have been tossed out the door to make room for tests, but this too, shall pass—"o-u-t- and in again." And when it comes back, the children will be there, greeting it with open arms.

Intery Mintery recorder players.

Intery Mintery dancers preparing to rise.

# EPILOGUE: POETRY AND MUSIC—A NEED FOR ALL AGES

I was giving a workshop in Australia when I got the call. My father had just had a heart attack and was going in for triple-bypass surgery—at 88 years old. I rushed home just in time to greet him when he awoke from surgery. It was a long six months of daily visits trying to coax him back to life, from hospital to rehab and finally to home. Ever hopeful that he would regain enough mobility to be somewhat self-sufficient, it finally became clear that he just didn't have the energy for it. He stopped eating and survived for a miraculous ten weeks before finally passing away.

We spent those ten weeks making the usual small talk—the latest news of his progress, who had visited, who had called or written. We talked of old times and family history, the news of the day and my daughters' plans for tomorrow. But some of our most moving moments were spent reciting poetry, listening to music and singing songs. My father astounded me by reciting much of the epic poem, *The Rime of the Ancient Mariner*, memorized in his early schooling.

Soon after, my mother moved into a nursing home. One day after rescuing her from a Bible class far over her head, I took her outside and recited a few rhymes from a book of jump rope chants I happened to have with me. She perked right up, delighted by the funny insults ("Roses are red, violets are green, my face is funny, but yours is a scream"), the image of Salome kicking the chandelier, and the sheer delight of rhythm and rhyme. I started reciting some of the old Mother Goose standards and she joined right in. Nursery rhymes gave her more solace and pleasure than the Bible.

Now when I visit her, I play old jazz standards on the piano and folks who can't speak a coherent sentence are singing along or mouthing the words. That music survives even the worst case of Alzheimer's has long been known, that people at the end of their life need music— to hear it, sing it, move however they can to it— is never questioned. As anyone in the geriatric profession can testify, it is as important for the old as it is for the young.

And so is poetry. Hear this plea from William Carlos Williams:

> My heart rouses
> thinking to bring you news
> of something
> that concerns you
> and concerns many men. Look at
> what passes for the news.
> You will not find it there but in
> despised poems.
> It is difficult
> to get the news from poems
> yet men die miserably every day

for lack
of what is found there.
Hear me out
for I too am concerned
and every man
who wants to die at peace in his bed
besides. *

How did something that brings so much meaning and enjoyment come to be "despised?" Puritanical fear of anything that animates the body, pleasures the senses, awakens Eros? Well, let the Puritans sit in their dusty corners and do penance however they like. For the rest of us, let the music flow! Let the poems be spoken! Let the dances be danced! Let the stories be told—dinner table stories, bedtime stories, campfire stories! Who says that to be an adult means to be serious, bring home just bacon and no cookies and milk, forego the frivolous fluff of art, and watch your spirit shrink day by day? Why can't we keep our child-like zest and sparkle alive amidst the hustle and bustle of adulthood?

Last year, some fifty neighbors went out to sing for our annual Christmas caroling party. A streetcar pulled up close to where we were gathered and I spontaneously climbed aboard with my accordion and asked the passengers if they had any requests. You can imagine the response— dead silence, no eye contact, a palpable uneasiness. I motioned to my fellow carolers to board and they swarmed on, walking down the aisles singing *Jingle Bells*. The driver smiled, closed the doors and off we went. For two short joyful blocks, the streetcar was alive with song. Even a few of the passengers joined in. Well, why not? People in cultures worldwide do sing on buses, dance in the street, recite poetry at the dinner table and play music their whole lives. What happened to us?

I've heard that brain-imaging technology reveals two human activities in which all parts of the brain are lit up—poetry and music. If we could map the heart, I imagine the result would be the same. A poet reciting, a singer singing, a cellist playing—they have the power to quiet a room, to make us listen as if our life depends on it. And maybe it does.

When a culture fails to immerse its children in these foundational experiences, when it cuts music programs, neglects poetry in the classroom and abandons children to video games and TV, a shadow falls across us all and the lingering effects darken the years. I sometimes wonder what this generation of children will do when they're in the nursing homes. With nothing but Britney Spears and Snoop Dog in their musical memories, how will they pass their days? Where will the beautiful songs and evocative stories and exquisite poems be when they need them? If we want to prepare our children for the future, let's look at their *whole* future. It's clear that rhymes and songs are vital for children fresh from the womb and equally vital for elders close to the tomb. Why not connect the dots and keep them alive our whole lives?

Schools are one place where we have the possibility of giving all children what they need today as children and what they will need tomorrow as adults. They are the bearers of the culture of the future—why not send them forth prepared with vision as well as skills? Dream with me here and imagine what kind of world children might create if…

…they read poems, wrote poems, recited poems, memorized poems each year of their
school life?

…they sang every day at school— songs of greeting, farewell, love, conflict, hope and triumph?

…they heard and read and told and enacted the old stories—Aesop's fables, Greek myths, Bible stories, fairy and folk tales from East and West, North and South—and began to read, write and tell the new ones?

---

* Excerpt from "Asphodel, That Greeny Flower"

…they danced and played the music of yesterday and then made their own dance and music
of today, from preschool through college?

What if all children in all schools started the day with a song or poem, ended the day with a story and danced in-between? What if all teachers committed themselves to these simple acts of filling their students' hearts with hope, their ears with beauty and their imaginations with stories that will feed them their whole lives? Then we might be at ease, knowing that we are sending our children into the promise of their future as Mother Goose would—

"with rings on their fingers and bells on their toes,

they shall have music wherever they go."

Children singing their way toward a bright future.

# INDEX

## ALPHABETICAL INDEX OF RHYMES

# INDEX BY SUGGESTED GRADE AND FOCUS

## INDEX BY MELODIC SCALE

### DO PENTATONIC

### RE PENTATONIC

### LA PENTATONIC

### SOL PENTATONIC

### MI PENTATONIC

### ALTERNATING DO/ LA

## ALTERNATING LA/ DO

## ALTERNATING DO/RE

## OTHER SCALES

## INDEX BY METER AND RHYTHM

## OTHER METERS

## SWING RHYTHM AND SYNCOPATION

## ANACRUSIS

## INDEX BY POETIC TYPE

# INDEX BY THEME

## FURTHER RESOURCES

- The American Orff Schulwerk Association: www.aosa.org
- The San Francisco International Orff Course: www.sforff.org
- Keith Terry Body Music: www.crosspulse.com

## SELECTED BIBLIOGRAPHY

Mother Goose collections are plentiful—the following collections and reflections on the tradition are some that I've particularly enjoyed:

Baring- Gould, William and Ceil: *The Annotated Mother Goose*; World Publishing Company, 1967
  The stories behind the rhymes, from political intrigue to social commentary.

Butler, Francelia: *Skipping Around the World: The Ritual Nature of Folk Rhymes*; Ballantine Books, NY
  A similar theme to the Opie's book below, investigating the ways in which children use rhymes to make sense of their world. With chapter titles like "Mystery and Romance; Hope and Hopelessness; Sex and Skipping," Ms Butler collects skipping rhymes from around the world (in English translations) and comments on them.

Carter, Robert: *The Tao of Mother Goose: Myth and Meaning in Nursery Rhymes*; Theosophical Publishing House, 1988
  A look behind the political meanings to mythological interpretations.

Goldstein, Bobbye S.: *Mother Goose on the Loose; Cartoons from the New Yorker*; Harry Abrams Inc. Pub.
  Treat yourself with this hilarious romp through cartoons inspired by Ma Goose.

Opie, Iona and Peter: *The Oxford Dictionary of Nursery Rhymes*: Oxford University Press, 1997
  The Opies are far and away the leading investigators and collectors of rhymes from the British Isles. This book is set up dictionary style "A was an apple pie" to "The Noble Duke of York," with fascinating commentary. A good resource book for teachers.

Opie, Iona, Wells, Rosemary: *Here Comes Mother Goose*; Candlewick Press 1999
  This one's for the kids, with delightful illustrations and large lettering.

Opie, Ioan and Peter. Sendak, Maurice: *I Saw Esau: The Schoolchild's Pocket Book*; Candlewick Press, 1992
  This collaboration with illustrator Maurice Sendak features rhymes from the school yard, grouped by themes like "Nonsense; Insults; Retaliation; Teasing: School Law; Counting out Rhymes" and other themes showing rhymes as survival mechanisms in a sometimes brutal kid's culture.

Roberts, Chris: *Heavy Words Lightly Thrown: The Reason Behind the Rhyme*; Gotham Books, 2004
  A delightful and readable commentary on the stories lurking behind the poems.

# ABOUT PENTATONIC PRESS

Pentatonic Press was formed by Doug Goodkin in 2004 with the following goals:

- To further the development of Orff Schulwerk through quality materials, ideas and processes grown from work with children of all ages.
- To attend to the roots of quality music education while exploring new territory.
- To provide a model of music and dance at the center of school curriculums, revealing their inherent connection with all subjects and their ability to cultivate community.
- To use music as a vehicle to reveal and cultivate each child's remarkable potential as an artist, citizen and compassionate human being.
- To offer full artistic control over the presentation of published material.

Pentatonic Press's growing catalogue includes nine published books and four CD's.

- THE ABC's OF EDUCATION: A Primer for Schools to Come—Doug Goodkin: 2006
- ALL BLUES: Jazz for the Orff Ensemble—Doug Goodkin: 2012
- BLUE IS THE SEA: Music, Dance & Visual Arts—Sofía López-Ibor: 2011
- BOOM CHICK-A-BOOM: Jazz for All Ages: Doug Goodkin & the Pentatonics (CD)
- FROM WIBBLETON TO WOBBLETON: Playing with Elements of Music and Movement—James Harding: 2013
- GANDAYINA: West African Xylophone Music (CD)
- INTERY MINTERY: Nursery Rhymes for Body, Voice & Orff Ensemble—Doug Goodkin: 2008
- KANBILE: SK Kakraba Lobi- Solo and Ensemble Xylophone Music of Ghana (CD)
- LOOKING AT THE ROOTS: A Guide to Understanding Orff Schulwerk—Wolfgang Hartmann: 2021
- NOW'S THE TIME: Teaching Jazz to All Ages—Doug Goodkin: 2004
- NOW'S THE TIME (Double CD)
- ORFF SCHULWERK IN DIVERSE CULTURES: An Idea That Went Round the World—Edited by Barbara Haselbach and Carolee Stewart: 2021
- TEACH LIKE IT'S MUSIC: An Artful Approach to Education—Doug Goodkin: 2019

Upcoming projects include such diverse subjects as guidelines for effective teaching, Ghana xylophone music, Ghanaian children's games, Balinese arts for children, jazz piano demystified and pentatonic, modal and harmonic music from the world repertoire for children.

Those interested in having their project considered can contact Doug through his website: www.douggoodkin.com

# ABOUT THE AUTHOR

Doug Goodkin is an internationally recognized Orff Schulwerk music teacher, teaching in over 50 countries worldwide. He worked with children from three years old to eighth grade in The San Francisco School for 45 years, is the author of nine books and writes a blog titled Confessions of a Traveling Music Teacher. He is also the pianist in the jazz quintet Doug Goodkin & the Pentatonics. His work has been described as "a long, earnest and continuing struggle to present music of integrity in a way that nurtures social justice and affirms our collective humanity."

For more information, go to www.douggoodkin.com